The LORD
from
HEAVEN

The LORD from HEAVEN

CHRISTIAN CLASSICS SERIES

*A study of the New Testament
teaching on the deity and humanity
of Jesus Christ*

by
Leon Morris

Inter-Varsity Press

INTER-VARSITY PRESS
38 De Montfort Street, Leicester LE1 7GP, England

© Inter-Varsity Press, 1958, 1974, 1995

Unless otherwise stated, quotations from the Bible are from the Revised
Standard Version, copyrighted 1946, 1952, © 1971, 1973, by the Division of
Christian Education, National Council of the Churches of Christ in the USA,
and used by permission.

First published 1958
Second edition 1974
First published in Christian Classics, 1995

British Library Cataloguing in Publication Data
A catalogue record for this book is available from the British Library.

ISBN 0-85111-234-X

Printed and bound in Great Britain by Cox and Wyman Ltd, Reading,
Berkshire.

*Inter-Varsity Press is the book-publishing division of the Universities and
Colleges Christian Fellowship (formerly the Inter-Varsity Fellowship), a
student movement linking Christian Unions in universities and colleges
throughout the United Kingdom and the Republic of Ireland, and a member
movement of the International Fellowship of Evangelical Students. For
information about local and national activities write to UCCF, 38, De Montfort
Street, Leicester LE1 7GP.*

Preface to the second edition

When a new edition of this little book was called for I was faced with a decision. I could have gone through it all thoroughly, updating its references to the literature and rewriting the whole in such a way as to reflect current discussions. But that would have been another book, and it is this one that has gone through several reprints and found its way into a number of languages. Clearly it has been meeting a need in this form. So I preferred to send it out again without extensive revision.

That does not mean that there are no changes. I have completely rewritten chapter 3 and some shorter sections here and there. The biblical quotations have been changed from the Authorized Version to the Revised Standard Version. And there are many minor changes in wording.

The basic reason that the book can go out in substantially the same form as the earlier edition is, of course, its subject-matter. It is not a high class (and dated) examination of a lot of modern writing, though there are some references to modern writers. It is nothing more pretentious than an attempt to bring out what the New Testament writers say in answer to the question, 'What do you think of the Christ?' As I said in the Preface to the first edition, 'The aim throughout has not been to clear up matters which are in dispute, but to set out what the New Testament has to say on the subject.' In my opinion that is just as important now as it was in 1958. The longer and more detailed works are essential for deep and serious study. But there is still a place for a little book which sets out shortly what the New Testament writers say about their Lord. It is my hope that this new edition will make the book useful to another circle of readers.

LEON MORRIS

Contents

Preface 5
1 Jesus of Nazareth 9
2 Jesus' view of Himself 25
3 Jesus the man 42
4 A Prince and a Saviour 55
5 The Lord of glory 67
6 A great High Priest 83
7 God the Word 93
8 Conclusion 107

1 Jesus of Nazareth

It was a tense moment.

The trouble with Thomas was that he was so sure of himself, and there was no getting an idea into his head at all. It was impossible for the other disciples not to be exasperated at his obstinate refusal to believe them. If they reflected that his attitude to them was much the same as their attitude to the women when they first heard of the resurrection, they probably felt that that was different. With lofty masculine scorn they had felt then that the women had been 'seeing things', and had not hesitated to dismiss their stories of angels and a risen Lord as nothing more than 'idle tales' (Lk. 24:11). But when ten superior males unanimously informed their colleague that Jesus was truly risen from the dead, for they had seen Him, he ought to have believed them.

They had argued with him, but he had not been persuaded. Incredibly, he saw no difference between believing them and believing the women! He did not know what had bewitched them, but he was firm in his refusal to accept what they said. He even laid down the terms on which he would believe: 'Unless I see in his hands the print of the nails, and place my finger in the mark of the nails, and place my hand in his side, I will not believe' (Jn. 20:25). There was no bearing with such a fellow.

For a week he had resisted them. And now they were all gathered together again, this time with Thomas among them. Suddenly, inexplicably, Jesus was in their midst, just as suddenly and inexplicably as on that previous occasion. Now

Thomas stood before his risen Lord. Would he believe? Would he really ask to put his finger in the print of the nails and his hand into the spear-wound? Would he try to explain away what he was now seeing as clearly as they?

The Lord invited His hard-headed servant to put Him to the test. 'Put your finger here,' He said, 'and see my hands; and put out your hand, and place it in my side; and do not be faithless, but believing' (Jn. 20:27). But there were limits to Thomas' doubts, and his moment of enlightenment issued in a leap of faith expressed in the joyous cry, 'My Lord and my God!' (Jn. 20:28).

'My Lord and my God.' It was not the first time that Jesus had been saluted as 'Lord', but this open ascription of full deity was something new. It represented the high point of faith in Jesus. Though it issued from a moment of sudden insight it came as the culmination of an impression that had been building up through all the days during which they had been associated. It was the response to the resurrection, but it was the resurrection of the Man whose life and death had left an indelible impression on the minds of His disciples.

Let us go back to the beginning.

Why did the disciples originally follow Jesus? The question is not an easy one to answer, for the Gospels give no indication that they had at first, nor for a long time afterwards, such an insight into His Person and message as would justify the far-reaching step they took. Their following of Him was not some shallow, half-hearted thing, such as often passes for Christianity in these days. They left their homes, their employment, their friends and relations, their familiar pursuits, all that had meant life to them, and were content to spend their days in journeys with Him about Galilee and elsewhere as He preached and taught the people about the Kingdom of God.

This teaching about the Kingdom may well have furnished the reason for their following Him in the first place. We know that the history of this period is studded with abortive attempts at revolt. Klausner, the Jewish historian, says of the period 67 BC–AD 39, 'Scarcely a year went by during this century without wars or other disturbances: wars, rebellions, outbreaks and riots.'[1] Men like Athronges, Judah the Galilean, Theudas, and many another raised up their tiny bands of followers and pitted themselves against the mightiest military machine the world had yet seen. Some acted blindly in unreasoning despair. Others, not totally devoid of military insight, realized that their pitiful little groups were no match for the mighty Roman legions. But with them patriotism and faith went hand-in-hand. They knew from the Scriptures that God reigns in the affairs of men, and they had come to the conclusion that God would in due course bring in His Kingdom. Then all the might of Rome or of any other military power would be swept away by the irresistible might of the Lord God omnipotent. And who could tell? It might be that Athronges, that Judah, that Theudas, was the chosen one, who, under the good hand of God, would lead His people to victory, and triumph over all the might of the Gentiles.

The Kingdom was in every man's thoughts. And Jesus came preaching the Kingdom. He made no attempt to enrol soldiers, but that would disconcert nobody at first. Other rebellions had been vitiated by premature action, and this simply meant that Jesus was minded not to rise before the right moment. In the meantime He was moving among the people, preaching, healing, becoming known, acquiring influence.

The teaching of Jesus

As He went about He ceaselessly preached the Kingdom. 'The kingdom of God is like a grain of mustard seed'; 'The kingdom of God –'; 'The kingdom of God –'; 'The kingdom –'. It was always on His lips. But as the days went by it began to dawn upon them that by 'the Kingdom' He did not mean quite what they meant. He never spoke of armies and battles and organization. Instead He said startling things like, 'Watch as you may, you will not *see* it come. People will not be saying, "Here it is!" or "There!" And the reason why is this – the Kingdom of God is within you' (Lk. 17:20f., Rieu's translation). How would He go about establishing a Kingdom like that?

[1] *Jesus of Nazareth* (London, 1928), p. 167.

They may well have been driven to reflect that the Aramaic word for 'kingdom' (like its Hebrew and Greek equivalents) does not mean so much a realm as a reign. We do well to be cautious here, for we can easily go astray by interpreting the Kingdom in terms of kingdoms we know. But the Bible idea is dynamic, not static. It is something that happens, not something that exists. It is a reign, a kingly rule, not a realm. It is God actively ruling in men's hearts.

This does not mean that the Kingdom is a piece of good advice, as though to say: 'Sin brings disaster. Live good lives, obey God, and so enter His Kingdom.' Jesus plainly recognized that men, of themselves, are only evil (Mk. 10:18; Lk. 11:13), and that if they are to live obediently to God's will they must be imbued with a power not their own. So He taught that the Kingdom is come in mighty power. Men are able to recognize it because demons are being cast out (Lk. 11:20). One stronger than the devil has come upon him and is spoiling him (Lk. 11: 21f.). That something more than moral reformation in a man's own strength is meant is hammered home with the story of the man out of whom went one devil, and into whom there presently entered seven others (Lk. 11:24–26). Jesus was not teaching men to pull themselves up by their own bootlaces, but pointing them to the power of God. The Kingdom of God is always miracle. Man 'knows not how' it grows (Mk. 4:26f.). Men may pray for it to come (Lk. 11:2), but it is a gift of God (Lk. 12:32). The idea that men should labour to bring in the Kingdom of God may be a noble ideal, but it is not the teaching of Scripture. The New Testament shows God breaking into this world of time and sense so that we see nothing less than the power of God Himself at work in the Kingdom which is set up in the work accomplished by Jesus.

This gives Jesus a very special place in the Kingdom, and by implication a very special relationship to God. The Kingdom is usually spoken of as God's, but on occasion it can be referred to as Jesus' Kingdom (Mt. 13:41; 16:28; 20:21; 25:34–40). Wrong relation to Him excludes men from the Kingdom, for that seems to be the sense of passages which speak of people knowing final rejection because of their attitude to Him (Mt.

7:23; Mk. 8:38). Continually He calls for allegiance to Himself personally (*e.g.* Mt. 10:37–39). One gets the impression from the Gospels that to be a follower of Jesus is to be in the Kingdom (*cf.* T. W. Manson, 'in the mind of Jesus, to become a genuine disciple of his and to enter into the Kingdom of God amounted to much the same thing'[1]).

This note of authority runs through all the teaching of Jesus. In our day we take it as a matter of course that a really great man will be original, but that was not the feeling of the men of the first century. To them it was an axiom that their fathers were wiser than they, and teachers were always careful to disclaim originality, and to show that what they put forward was the teaching of the ancients. When a truly original teacher did arise he had to resort to great ingenuity to fasten his teaching on to some illustrious predecessor to gain a hearing.

But Jesus did no such thing. It is often said today that His teaching was not very original, and that almost all of it can be paralleled from the teachings of the Rabbis. This is true, but only within limits. If you search the immense field of Rabbinic literature you will find somewhere or other parallels sometimes more, sometimes less exact to much of the teaching of Jesus. But it is an immense field, and the remark attributed to Jülicher, 'It is a pity they said so much else,' is very much to the point. Well might Bousset say, 'the Rabbis stammered, but Jesus spoke.'[2] There is none of the Rabbis who has anything like the range or the comprehension or the spirit of Jesus. As Scott Lidgett has said: 'The originality of our Lord is to be found in the body of His teaching, as an organic whole held together by great vitalising principles.'[3] It is true that parallels may be found to many of the individual sayings, but it is not true that any parallel can be found to the general impression left by the teaching of Jesus. The Rabbis spoke *from* authority, Jesus *with* authority. Those who heard Him 'were astonished at his teaching, for he taught them as one that had authority, and not

1 *The Teaching of Jesus* (Cambridge, 1943), p. 206.
2 Cited by H. E. W. Turner in *Jesus, Master and Lord* (London, 1953), p. 135.
3 *The Spiritual Principle of the Atonement* (London, 1914), p. 20.

as the scribes' (Mk. 1:22. C. H. Dodd renders 'He taught them like a sovereign, and not like the Rabbis'[1]). W. Manson reminds us that the word rendered 'authority' in the Hellenistic world 'implied supernatural power' and he cites the saying of Justin Martyr, 'His word was power from God.'[2] 'Thus says the Lord' is typical of the Old Testament, but Jesus' characteristic expression is 'Truly, truly, I say to you'. The difference is significant. Jesus appealed to no other authority as He spoke to men of the deep things of God.

In conclusion, let us look at the incident in John 7. The enemies of Jesus sent officers to arrest Him as He was teaching in the temple courts. There was a crowd, and the men could not perform their task in a moment. Before they could push their way through the press they caught something of what He was saying, their attention was gripped, and they remained to listen enthralled. Presently they returned to those that had sent them, but without their Prisoner. Asked why they had failed to perform the arrest they answered simply, 'No man ever spoke like this man!' (Jn. 7:46). Of course they did not mean that His teaching proved Him to be divine, but we may well ask whether their statement may not be pressed in this way. When we consider His position in the Kingdom and the authority of His statements and when we note His intimate knowledge of the nature of God and the reaction of His hearers, surely we must ask the question, Is not such a Teacher something more than a man?

The personality of Jesus

We can quite easily miss the impact of the personality of Jesus, taken up as we are with traditions of the 'Gentle Jesus, meek and mild' variety. It is true that Jesus manifested gentleness and meekness, but this is the compassion of the strong, and not the impotence of the weak. I think that many people have the impression that Jesus was rather negative, a quiet, withdrawing

1 *Mysterium Christi*, ed. G. K. A. Bell and A. Deissmann (London, 1930), p. 56.
2 *Jesus the Messiah* (London, 1944), p. 35.

type of person, who told beautiful stories and did not retaliate when He was ill-treated.

This is true in a way, but it gives a false impression. Jesus was dynamic. His was a personality that gripped men. Let me quote from Beverley Nichols' reply to the radical French scholar, Prof. Guignebert:

'... all he will admit, in his most generous moment, is that "the outline of a man and the traces of an individual activity are still to be distinguished".

'Ye gods! If you have ever done any writing you may have a faint idea of the immense difficulty of making a character *live* even for a single publishing season, in a single language. And if you have ever done any reading, the remotest acquaintance with European literature will inform you that there are no "characters", not even Don Quixote (the most lifelike evocation of an individual in literature) which are more than tiny shadows against the immense reality of the character of Jesus.

'You cannot deny the reality of this character, *in whatever body it resided*. Even if we were to grant the Professor's theory that it is all a hotch-potch of legend, *somebody* said "The Sabbath was made for man, and not man for the Sabbath"; *somebody* said "For what shall it profit a man if he shall gain the whole world and lose his own soul"; *somebody* said "Suffer the little children to come unto me, and forbid them not: for of such is the Kingdom of God"; *somebody* said "How hardly shall they that have riches enter into the Kingdom of God"; *somebody* said "All they that take the sword shall perish with the sword".

'*Somebody* said these things, because they are staring me in the face at this moment from the Bible. And whoever said them was *gigantic*. And whoever said them was *living*, because we are in the year 1936 and I am "modern" and you are "modern", and we both of us like going to the cinema and we can both drive a car and all that sort of thing, and yet we cannot find in any contemporary literature any phrases which have a shadow of the beauty, the truth, the individuality, nor the *indestructibility* of those phrases.

'And remember, I have only quoted five sentences at at random.'[1]

Yes, Jesus was gigantic. There was nothing trite or commonplace about His words, and there was nothing colourless about His deeds. Consider the forcefulness of the personality of One who made a whip of small cords and single-handed drove the greedy traders out of the temple precincts (Jn. 2:13ff.). Or of One who so awed a crowd of excited Galileans, thirsting for His blood and about to hurl Him over a precipice, that He simply walked through the middle of the crowd and went on His way.

Or think of the devotion He inspired. It wasn't simply that men and women rather liked Him. They left their homes, their friends, their means of livelihood and simply followed Him wherever He went. We are used to a feeble and tepid thing masquerading as Christian service these days; but those first followers of Christ were very much in earnest. For them following Jesus meant literally giving up all things. But they did it with joy, counting all well lost for Him. Men and women alike came to see in Him their all in all. There were impulsive people like Peter, and visionaries like John. There were hardheaded people like Levi the tax-collector and inveterate doubters like Thomas. There were people like Andrew with a wonderful way of winning people and bringing them to his Master. There was Philip, dull and rather slow of understanding, and Simon the Zealot, energetic and ardently patriotic, with many more beside. People of every walk of life came to Him, people of widely differing temperament and intelligence, the hasty and the cautious, the brainy and the dull. Some came openly, and some, like Nicodemus, came in secret.

In the second half of the twentieth century there is no need to labour the point that almost anyone can get a following of some sort. But Jesus drew men and women of all kinds. And

[1] *The Fool Hath Said* (London, 1936), pp. 126f. (Nichols' italics). Quoted by kind permission of the publishers, Messrs Jonathan Cape Ltd.

not only did He draw them: He held them and inspired them. They were transformed by His touch, so that they never went back again to the life they lived before they gave Him their allegiance. As they came into close touch with Jesus they came into close touch with God, and their lives were permanently enriched by the experience. E. A. Knox put it this way: 'there has been no other instance, nor will there be another, of one whose Personality, without effort, without self-assertion, without the barest suspicion of megalomania, it would seem almost without direct claim, left upon His immediate entourage the solemn conviction that they had been walking with God.'[1]

The miracles

If the Gospels are at all reliable Jesus on occasion did things which we can only describe as miracles. They do not fit into the character of natural happenings, as we know them. These cannot be excised from the Gospels. In the limited number of incidents recorded in the life of Jesus the proportion of miracles is surprisingly high.

In early times the miracles were eagerly put forward as evidence of the deity of Christ and of the truth of Christianity. But in more recent years there has been a sense of embarrassment, a feeling that somehow the miracles discredit the faith, and that they must be explained away lest the whole of Christianity be thought to be nothing but legend. There came a vogue of finding 'natural' explanations for some of the miracles, and of denying the rest. Later again, a tendency emerged to think of them as a more or less human activity. Thus D. M. Baillie speaks of 'one particularly fruitful insight that has been gained in the modern world . . . that the problem of the "mighty works" can be disposed of neither by denying them out of hand as unhistorical, nor by accepting them as sheerly supernatural portents because a divine Christ can do anything, but is to be met only by regarding them as works of faith, wrought by the power of God in response to human faith for which all things are possible',[2] and he goes on to say, 'the

1 *The Glad Tidings of Reconciliation* (London, 1916), p. 2.
2 *God Was in Christ* (London, 1948), p. 13.

"powers of the world to come" were at the disposal of *all* who would believe. God had given such power *to men*.'[1] D. S. Cairns has argued the point at length in *The Faith that Rebels*. Leonard Hodgson says that we must 'think of the powers exercised by Christ as being powers open to manhood where manhood is found in its perfection'.[2]

Now it may well be that insufficient attention has been given to the way in which Christ steadfastly refused to work that kind of miracle which would simply be a display of divine power, and indeed, regarded it as a temptation of the devil. He does not appear in the pages of the Gospels as a wonder-worker. The miracles are not explicitly cited to show that here was One who was more than man. So much may readily be conceded. But at the same time it is clear that the miracles are not regarded as commonplace, as the sort of thing which any man can do, or perhaps might do were he more righteous. Nothing in the Gospels points us to such a conclusion. The miracles are something special. They 'are a demonstration from God that what prophets and righteous men had desired to see is at hand and already in process'.[3]

Nor are modern men right when they maintain that the miracles were wrought only in response to faith. There are three accounts, for example, of the healing of Simon's wife's mother (Mt. 8:14f.; Mk. 1:29–31; Lk. 4:38f.), and faith is mentioned in none of them. Nor is it in the account which follows of the healing of 'all who were sick or possessed with demons' (Mk. 1:32). Are we to think that the whole multitude was suitably pious? Faith is not mentioned in the case of the Gadarene demoniac (Mt. 8:28–34; Mk. 5:1–20; Lk. 8:26–39), nor of the woman bowed together (Lk. 13:10–17), nor of the widow of Nain's son (Lk. 7:11–17), nor the lame man at Bethesda (Jn. 5:1–9), nor a number of others.

In some cases it may fairly be said that faith is implied, but by no means in all. For example, there seems no place for it in

[1] *Op. cit.*, p. 14 (Baillie's italics).
[2] *And Was Made Man* (London, 1933), p. 133.
[3] W. Manson, *op. cit.*, p. 34.

the case of Malchus (Lk. 22:50f.), and it seems expressly excluded in the raising of Lazarus, where nobody looked for the miracle, even up to the time of Martha's protest at the opening of the grave. The man at the pool of Bethesda seems to have been an unpleasant type (on learning who it was who had healed him he promptly betrayed Jesus to the Jews, knowing that they were incensed at what they held to be a breach of the Sabbath), and the narrative gives no hint of faith. If we are to remain biblical in our understanding of the miracles we must say that, while faith was commonly antecedent to cures, Jesus was not limited in His mighty works by men. And, of course, if this is so in the case of healings, it is all the more so with the nature miracles, like the feeding of the multitudes and the stilling of the storm.

Some have objected to the whole concept of miracle on the grounds of its irrelevancy. Matthew Arnold is said to have asked what possible evidence of authority is shown by a man turning into a pen-wiper before one's eyes. Exactly. But there are no miracles of that kind in the Bible, though we may find them in plenty in the non-canonical writings, *e.g.* the Infancy Gospels. In the New Testament the miracles are not so much 'portents' (*teras*, the Greek word conveying this meaning, is used of Christ's miracles only in Acts 2:22), as 'signs'. The word is important. The miracles of Christ point us to God. The people who saw them reacted as in the presence of God. They were amazed at the authority they revealed (Mk. 1:27), they glorified God (Mt. 9:8), they were afraid ('awe-struck', Mt. 9:8, RV), they were filled with fear ('awe' again, Lk. 5:26), they recognized a divine visitation (Lk. 7:16), they were astonished at the majesty of God (Lk. 9:43).

It is not easy to resist the conclusion that the One who gave these signs was divine. On one occasion He performed a miracle explicitly to show that He had power to forgive sins (Mk. 2:10ff.), while He sometimes thought of miracles as a means of eliciting faith in Himself. Although this is not the highest kind of faith, Jesus did not despise it (Jn. 5:36). As Bernard says, 'The highest faith is that which can believe without a sign (xx.29), but signs have a useful function as bearing their witness to the glory of Jesus.'[1] Jesus even rebuked people for following Him because they were fed, and *not* because of the miracles (Jn. 6:26). In a saying recorded in Matthew 11:4f. and Luke 7:20–22 (ascribed by source critics to Q, which is regarded as perhaps the very oldest Christian writing) Jesus appealed to the miracles as accrediting Him.

Those who object to the way miracles have been handled in the past have at least this to be said for their point of view: the miracles are not something extra, something added to the revelation in order to accredit it. They are part of the revelation.[2] We see the Kingdom of God in the fact that mighty powers are in operation (Lk. 11:20). They are not devices to which God had to resort when He could not do what He wished by normal means, but part of His plan. Someone has said that if a stone is cast into a pool a piscatorial observer might discern all sorts of 'miracles', the casting up of spray, the setting of wavelets in motion, the striking of a slow tadpole, the stirring up of mud on the bottom, and so, according to the 'laws' of the pool, they are. But they are the inevitable consequences of the irruption of a body from outside. So with Christ. What we term 'miracle' is His way of working. When we have the entry of a Being of a different order into the human sphere of life we must expect to see happenings which cannot be explained by the laws governing human conduct. And those happenings are part of the evidence which indicates that such an entry has, in fact, occurred.

The sinlessness of Jesus
On one occasion Jesus asked His enemies, 'Which of you convicts me of sin?' (Jn. 8:46), and nobody took up the challenge. His enemies accused Him of many things. Yet they do not seem to have disputed the claim that He lived sinlessly. There is nothing that can be called sin in the accusations that they brought against Him.

[1] *The Gospel According to St John (ICC)*, on Jn. 2 : 11.
[2] *Cf.* Alan Richardson, who says that miracles are 'part of the proclamation of the Kingdom of God: as such they are designed to awaken, not wonder, but repentance.' *A Theological Word Book of the Bible* (London, 1950), p. 154.

If anything, it is even more surprising that the friends of Jesus record no fault in Him, for the Twelve were with Him constantly. It is comparatively easy to give a good impression when we are making only occasional contacts, as our proverb, 'Street angel, house devil!' reminds us. Many people who are very pleasant to outsiders may be a great trial to those who have to live with them. In the home, in the day-by-day contacts, where there is no need to keep up appearances, all manner of faults show up that are not visible elsewhere. The home is the test. But these men, who lived with Jesus constantly, day and night, throughout the period of His ministry never spoke of observing any kind of sin in Him.

This testimony is airily dismissed by those who say, 'But the only information there is is contained in the Gospels, and they are hopelessly biased. The evangelists simply told all the good things about their Hero, and kept quiet about the rest!'

To this many things could be replied. In the first place it is worth pointing out that the Gospels give no evidence of viewing life through rose-tinted spectacles. When the evangelists looked back to those days they remembered the faults and faithfully recorded them. Though Peter was widely revered as a very great apostle his threefold denial of the Master is recorded in each Gospel.

Similarly it is recorded that James and John were rebuked for wanting to call down fire on unfriendly Samaritans. The evangelists reveal that the apostles quarrelled on the very eve of the crucifixion as to which of them should be the greatest. The failings of the little band are there to be read by all.

Again, the Gospels never praise Jesus. I do not think there is one word of praise for the Master in any one of the four Gospels from start to finish. The evangelists simply record what happened, and let it go at that. How they did it I do not know. I think it would be very difficult for any Christian today, or for that matter in any age, to compose a writing about Jesus the length of a Gospel and never for one moment slip into praise. Yet this the four evangelists did.

Moreover, the Jesus of the Gospels does not conform to first-century specifications for a hero, either Jewish or Gentile.

Otto Borchert has shown how, at point after point, Jesus was a stumbling-block to men of His day, displaying qualities they reprobated, and despising what they rated highly as virtues.[1] Had the evangelists depicted a Jesus of their own making we would have a very different figure.

It is also worth noting that we are not helpless in detecting faults in the great ones of the past, even when we owe our information to adulatory biographies. Take as an example the apocryphal story of Judith. The enemy, led by Holofernes, advanced on the people of Judea, and encamped about Bethulia, the city where Judith lived. They took the water springs, and so desperate were the circumstances of the besieged that the rank and file compelled the leaders to agree to surrender at the end of five days if deliverance had not come within that time. Judith, a young widow of great beauty, rebuked the elders for their pusillanimity and want of faith and proclaimed that the Lord would deliver them by her hand.

Arrayed in her finery she went down with her maid to the camp of the enemy. There she exercised all her feminine wiles to beguile Holofernes. The infatuated general completely succumbed to her charms. On the fourth day of her stay he made her a great feast which lasted until the evening. Alone with him, Judith made him drunk, and when he was helpless cut off his head. She returned with it to her own people who, of course, launched an attack, and the enemy were no little disconcerted to find themselves 'headless'. The men of Judea won a resounding victory.

There is no doubt that the writer has given us a noble story. There is no doubt either that he thought much of his heroine. She was beautiful, she was courageous, she was resourceful. We, too, can admire her, but we cannot ignore that she was a liar, an assassin, and one or two other unpleasant things as well. From our more developed standpoint we discern flaws even in the portrait painted by one concerned only to display her perfections. And the same is true of all other great ones of the past. Of course, this is not the way to appreciate them. It is

[1] *The Original Jesus* (London, 1936), especially Part I.

not fair to judge a man or woman except by the standards of their own day.

But in the case of Jesus of Nazareth it does not matter. Let the standard be that of the first or of the twentieth century, He still remains sinless. I do not mean that the captious cannot find something on which to fasten. Someone has complained that He could not be perfect who cursed the fig tree for not bearing fruit out of season. This is to forget our ignorance of much of the circumstances, and the fact that the incident appears to be an acted parable. Let those bent on criticism make what they can of such things. To fair-minded men it seems clear that the record does not convict Jesus of sin in any matter.

It should also be borne in mind that the greatest saints have always been the most conscious of their sin. The greater their sanctity, the greater their sense of sin. Indeed their tender consciences are a big factor in their moral achievement. But although He called on others to repent, there is no record of Jesus setting an example. 'That which overawes us is the manifest combination of utter sincerity with utter cloudlessness of conscience.'[1] He never sought the Father's forgiveness. 'He was certainly without the gratitude of the redeemed sinner!'[2]

Now a sinless man is a unique phenomenon. It is the way of men to sin, and the sinlessness of Jesus cries out for explanation. We would not wish to assert that His sinlessness arose from some automatic necessity of His nature which placed Him above temptation. He was tempted, sorely tempted. Indeed, in the lights of James 1:13, this forms a considerable part of the evidence for the reality of His manhood. Nor would we wish to deny the truth contained in William Temple's words: 'He overcame them (i.e. temptations) exactly as every man who does so overcomes a temptation – by the constancy of the Will.'[3] But we maintain that, when full allowance has been made for all this, the sinlessness of Jesus demands an explanation, and the idea that He was no more than a man does not give one. As Stevens says: 'It is open to the radical theologian to say that the

[1] E. A. Knox, *op. cit.*, p. 100.
[2] Otto Borchert, *op. cit.*, p. 213.
[3] *Christus Veritas* (London, 1925), p. 147.

positing of a metaphysical union with God as the basis of the unique consciousness and character of Jesus is a subsequent explanation which Paul and John have given. But it *is* an explanation, and the mere assertion that Jesus' consciousness was "purely human" *is not*. It is, moreover, an explanation which these apostles base upon the teaching and life of Jesus as they knew them.'[1] So with the sinlessness of Jesus. If this points us to deity well and good. But if not, how shall we account for it?

This, then, is the kind of picture the Gospels give us. It is not the whole picture, and indeed, some of the more important evidence is being left for the next chapter. But as the apostles journeyed with Jesus of Nazareth, His personality, His intimate knowledge of the inmost nature of God, the authoritative teaching that He gave in the deep things of God, the miracles that He wrought as naturally as He breathed (if not as easily, Mk. 5:30), the sinless life lived out before them, all these combined to make the deepest of impressions upon them. Small wonder that at the climax of it all Thomas should cry, 'My Lord and my God!'

1 *The Theology of the New Testament* (Edinburgh, 1901), p. 64.

2 Jesus' view of Himself

'Jesus was a good man. The theologians have spoiled things by making Him a god. More's the pity!' So runs the modern dictum. Men do not like the supernatural, so they deny its existence or minimize its scope. But for all the popularity of the idea it cannot be derived from the Gospels. If we are to take our understanding of the Person of Jesus from these sources we cannot think of Him in such terms. Let us look at the records in more detail.

The Son of man

Jesus' favourite self-designation was 'the Son of man'. This expression occurs over eighty times in the Gospels, and the intriguing thing is that it is always on the lips of Jesus. Stephen used it once (Acts 7:56), and the people once asked whom Jesus meant by it; but these are the only recorded occasions when anyone used it of the Master other than Jesus Himself. But He used it constantly. It is found in all four Gospels, and in all the sources which New Testament critics postulate behind the Gospels. There seems no reason for denying that Jesus used it of Himself, or that He used it often. No other self-designation seems to have appealed to Him so much.

The passages in which 'the Son of man' occurs divide into three classes. In the first, the term is used generally of Christ's earthly ministry. It seems to be simply a periphrasis for 'I', as when Jesus said, 'Foxes have holes, and the birds of the air have nests; but the Son of man has nowhere to lay his head'

25

(Mt. 8:20). A second group of passages speaks of a heavenly Son of man, and of the glory of Christ at His second coming. 'And then they will see the Son of man coming in clouds with great power and glory' (Mk. 13:26). The third group by contrast speaks of the Son of man as suffering. 'And he began to teach them that the Son of man must suffer many things, and be rejected by the elders and the chief priests and the scribes, and be killed, and after three days rise again' (Mk. 8:31).

'The Son of man' is not a very natural expression in Greek. It is a slavishly literal rendering of the Aramaic *bar-nasha*, which would more naturally be rendered by 'man' or 'the man'. Some accordingly have suggested that the term does not really denote Jesus, but man in general. Such explanations are inadequate. While some passages might be explained in this way, the great majority will not lend themselves to this treatment. None of the three quoted in the last paragraph, for example, can refer to mankind at large. They refer to Jesus personally, and the same is true of the Son of man passages in general.

A better line of approach is that which goes back to the Old Testament for examples of the use of the term. The prophet Ezekiel is frequently addressed as 'son of man', and there are some Psalms which employ the expression (*e.g.* Ps. 8 : 4). But close attention to these parts of Scripture shows that the term is used to emphasize man's weakness and dependence as a creature. While this would fit in with some of the Gospel passages it is out of harmony with others, in particular with those which speak of the glory of the Son of man. Few scholars have maintained that Jesus' use of the expression is derived from Ezekiel or the Psalms.[1]

More see its origin in the heavenly Son of man in Daniel 7. The prophet 'saw in the night visions, and behold, with the clouds of heaven, there came one like a son of man, and he came to the Ancient of Days, and was presented before him. And to him was given dominion and glory and kingdom, that all peoples, nations, and languages, should serve him; his do-

[1] But there have been some, for example J. Y. Campbell and G. S. Duncan.

minion is an everlasting dominion, which shall not pass away, and his kingdom one that shall not be destroyed' (Dn. 7: 13f.). The dominant idea is that of sovereignty. The Son of man rules with divine authority. This needs some emphasis, for in our day 'Son of man' is often used to show Christ's humanity, over against 'Son of God', which refers to His deity. The truth is that 'Son of man' is a title pointing to deity rather than humanity.

Later in Daniel 7 we read, 'And the kingdom and the dominion, and the greatness of the kingdoms under the whole heaven, shall be given to the people of the saints of the Most High; their kingdom shall be an everlasting kingdom' (verse 27). These words so strongly resemble those of verses 13f. that some have felt that 'one like the Son of man' is simply a way of symbolizing 'the people of the saints of the Most High'. While this is probably going too far, yet the Son of man is closely associated with a people. He is a societary figure. T. W. Manson has emphasized this aspect of the Son of man; for example, he says, 'His (i.e. Jesus') mission is to create the Son of Man, the Kingdom of the saints of the Most High, to realize in Israel the ideal contained in the term.'[1] Not many scholars go all the way with Manson, but clearly the connection between the Son of man and the saints of the Most High is close.

The heavenly Son of man is not referred to again in the Old Testament. He is spoken of in the Similitudes of Enoch (i.e., chapters 37–71 of the Ethiopian Book of Enoch), an apocryphal writing of uncertain date. While many scholars think the Similitudes pre-Christian (e.g. R. H. Pfeiffer), others regard them as a Christian interpolation into the original Jewish book. We cannot use them with confidence as the source of Jesus' use of the term. The most we can say is that if the section is genuine it indicates that the term 'Son of man' as used in Daniel 7 was sometimes used also in later Jewish circles. But C. H. Dodd says, 'the Similitudes are in any case an isolated and probably eccentric authority for the association of the title "Son of Man" with an "apocalyptic Messiah", and cannot be used with any confidence to elucidate the New Testament.'[2]

[1] *The Teaching of Jesus* (Cambridge, 1943), p. 227.
[2] *According to the Scriptures* (London, 1953), pp. 116f.

Why then did Jesus adopt this term? We might answer, firstly because it was a rare term and one without nationalistic associations. It would lead to no political complications. 'The public would . . . read into it as much as they apprehended of Jesus already, and no more.'[1] Secondly, because it had overtones of divinity. J. P. Hickinbotham goes as far as to say, 'the Son of Man is a title of divinity rather than humanity.'[2] Thirdly, because of its societary implications. The Son of man implies the redeemed people of God. Fourthly, because it had undertones of humanity. He took upon Him our weakness.

The Messiah

The Jews looked for the coming of a great One whom they called the Messiah. This is our transliteration of a Hebrew word which means 'anointed'. Translated into Greek it is *Christos*, from which we get 'Christ'. But the idea remains Jewish, not Greek. 'It is doubtful whether such an expression as *ho christos* would have conveyed any meaning at all to a Greek.'[3] In the Old Testament the king was spoken of as 'the Lord's anointed', and the priest as 'the anointed priest'. Prophets may also have been anointed. (In 1 Kings 19: 16 Elijah is told to anoint Elisha as prophet, though there is no record of this being carried out.) The significance of anointing appears to have been the consecrating of the person anointed to a particular religious task, perhaps also the enduement with divine grace for the task. This was so even in the case of the king, for he ruled not absolutely, in his own right, but as one deputed by God to perform this task.

The Messiah, then, was one who was expected to come; in a very special way He would set forward God's purposes. There was more than one concept of Messiahship, but it would be true to say that by the first century the Jews had come to look on the Messiah as someone in a special relationship to God. He would usher in the end of the age, when the kingdom of

[1] R. H. Fuller, *The Mission and Achievement of Jesus* (London, 1954), p. 106.

[2] *The Churchman*, April-June, 1944, p. 54.

[3] Jackson and Lake, *The Beginnings of Christianity*, 1 (London, 1920), p. 347.

God would be established. Many prophecies of the Scripture were applied to Him, and all in all He was of divine stature. As Gregory Dix has said, 'The *function* of the Messiah is a Divine function; His bringing in the "Kingdom of the Heavens" is God's own bringing in of His own Kingdom. . . . Once Jesus was accepted as "Messiah" by Jews (even by Himself as a Jew) this identification of His own action in history with the action of God Himself was *inescapable*.'[1]

'Messiah' so exactly expresses what Jesus was and came to do that we naturally wonder why He did not use this category to characterize His mission. The answer probably lies in the way it was interpreted by the Jews of His day. For them the Messiah was, in one aspect at least, a political deliverer. They looked to Him to lead their armies against the hated Roman overlord, and to establish such a mighty empire as the world had never yet seen, an empire with its capital at Jerusalem, an empire world-wide in its scope, an empire in which God was supreme. Jesus decisively rejected this whole idea. For Him the suggestion that He should establish such an empire was nothing less than a temptation of the devil.

Thus to announce Himself as the Messiah would have been to invite misunderstanding. Every Jew who heard the term would be thinking in terms of eventual rebellion against Rome, and of the glorious consummation when the Jewish Empire would replace the Roman. At the same time Jesus did not reject the true concept of Messiahship. He knew Himself to be the Messiah, and on occasion could avow this, as in John's account of His talk with the woman of Samaria, or when Mark reports His words about giving 'a cup of water to drink because you bear the name of Christ' (Mk. 9:41). He raised no objection to the use of the term by Peter (Mk. 8:29), or by Caiaphas (Mk. 14:61), though in each case in His reply He used the expression 'the Son of man'. It is as though He felt that in some sense the word could be used of Him, but everything depended on the content put into it. His reply to Peter is most illuminating, stressing as it does that 'the Son of man must suffer many things' (Mk. 8:31). Some have felt that the passages where Jesus

[1] *Jew and Greek* (London, 1953), p. 80 (Dix's italics).

accepted Messiahship may easily be excised from the Gospels, and that Jesus never thought of Himself in Messianic terms. This cannot be sustained, however, for the Messianic claim is implicit in many places, *e.g.* the temptation narratives, and the reply of Jesus to the messengers of John the Baptist (Lk. 7: 19–22). On no occasion did He reject this title. Moreover, as Otto points out, 'He was crucified as a Messianic claimant and without the Messianic claim the crucifixion of Christ is meaningless. The fact that he was crucified proves that he did not want to clear himself of the suspicion of being claimant to Messiahship, and therefore that he confirmed this claim before the procurator.'[1]

Of particular importance is the way in which Jesus insisted on the lowly aspect of His Messiahship. The temptation narratives at the beginning of His ministry show Him rejecting the temptations to use His miraculous powers to make stones into bread, to perform miracles that were merely spectacular, and to set up an earthly kingdom. He discerned the voice of Satan in each of these suggestions, and He turned from them. What Messiahship meant for Him is clearly brought out in the account of Peter's great confession at Caesarea Philippi. Jesus had asked the disciples who men thought Him to be, and, after various answers, asked them who they thought He was. Peter replied: 'You are the Christ, the Son of the living God' (Mt. 16:16; Mk. 8:29 has 'You are the Christ', and Lk. 9:20, 'The Christ of God'). This is the first time that any of His followers had penetrated into the secret of His Person, and Jesus attributed it to nothing less than a revelation from God the Father (Mt. 16: 17). The immediate sequel is important. 'From that time Jesus began to show his disciples that he must go to Jerusalem and suffer many things from the elders and chief priests and scribes, and be killed, and on the third day be raised.' From the time that they knew Him to be the Messiah (Christ) He began to instruct them in the necessity for the passion. So far from Messiahship for Jesus meaning the path of eminence and

---

[1] *The Kingdom of God and the Son of Man* (London, 1943), pp. 228f. Sir Edwyn Hoskyns, in his valuable essay in *Mysterium Christi*, has demonstrated conclusively the centrality of the Messianic concept.

authority and ease, it meant the way of suffering and shame and death. He had come to perform the divine function of seeking and saving the lost (Lk. 19:10), and that involved death, the death which would be a ransom for many (Mk. 10:45). Jesus thought of Messiahship as following a lowly path, but this should not mislead us into thinking that He thought little of His Person. Rather the reverse is the case. Petty human minds might think in terms of earthly empires and material glory. The divine mind of Christ thought in terms of the salvation of men through the way of the cross.

The Servant

Of particular importance is His application of the concept of the Suffering Servant of Isaiah 53 to His mission. He does not often apply this passage explicitly to Himself (an exception is Lk. 22: 37) but all commentators are agreed that an allusion is frequently to be detected. 'Though He never uses the actual words, the title "Servant of the Lord" often trembles on His lips.'[1] See, for example, Mark 8:31; 10:45; Luke 19:10; 22:27, etc.

Now the essence of the mission of the Suffering Servant is that He suffers, but through His sufferings others are blessed. Apply this to the work of Jesus, and, as W. Manson puts it, 'He who is called to be the Messiah-Son of God sees the way marked out for him by the practice of the Servant, and teaches also that only through the humiliation and self-sacrifice of the Servant is the glory of the Son of Man to be attained.'[2]

It has often been pointed out that the combination of the heavenly Son of man with the lowly Suffering Servant is a striking paradox. Jesus did not yield in the slightest His claim to the very highest position of all. But He understood that that involved being the Servant of those He came to save. This point is strikingly exemplified in the crescendo of Mark 10: 43-45.

The Son of God

We have come to take the Fatherhood of God so much for granted that we tend to overlook the revolutionary nature of

[1] A. M. Hunter, *The Work and Words of Jesus* (London, 1950), p. 80.
[2] *Jesus the Messiah* (London, 1944), p. 111.

Jesus' handling of this theme. He constantly referred to God simply as 'Father' or 'My Father'. Jews of that day were careful to include the adjective 'heavenly', and they usually said 'our heavenly Father'. In prayer they used the form of address '*Abhi*' ('My Father') as a rule adding 'in heaven'. This form was no longer employed in the intimacy of the family circle, where the earthly father was addressed as '*Abba*'. But Jesus used '*Abba*' in prayer (Mk. 14:36. Scholars are agreed that this Aramaic underlies the Greek in other places also). The daring of this is that 'the usage of family life is transferred to God: it is the language of the child to its father'.[1] Jesus treated God as familiarly as a child treats its father.

Jesus taught men to think of God as Father in an intimate way, but He did not give the impression that God was His Father in the same sense as theirs. He called God 'my Father' (Mt. 11:27; Lk. 2:49), or 'your Father' (Mt. 5:16, 45; Lk. 12:30). He used 'Our Father' only in giving the Lord's prayer as a pattern, a prayer which He Himself did not pray. He seemed to go out of His way to avoid saying 'our Father', as in John 20:17, 'I am ascending to my Father and your Father'. This is all the more striking in that 'our Father' was the common Jewish expression. Nowhere does He give countenance to the idea that He and others are in the same sense 'sons of God'. The Jews understood the way in which He claimed God as Father to mean that He was making Himself 'equal with God' (Jn. 5:18).

Though He rarely used the expression 'Son of God' (never in the Synoptic Gospels), it is clear that He thought of Himself as God's Son. We have already noted the special relationship to the Father which He claimed, and, in addition, He sometimes spoke of Himself as 'the Son', as, for example, in Matthew 11:27 and Mark 13:32. The former passage is so much like many passages in the Fourth Gospel that it has been described as 'a Synoptic bolt from the Johannine blue'. Since it is unique in the Synoptic Gospels its genuineness in whole or in part has been contested. There seems, however, no reason why we should not accept the saying. There are no objective grounds, textual or otherwise, for excising it, and most modern scholars recognize

[1] G. Dalman, *The Words of Jesus* (Edinburgh, 1902), p. 192.

that subjectively there is more to be said for it than against it. Its importance is that it explicitly places Jesus in such a relationship to God as is shared by no man: 'no one knows the Son except the Father, and no one knows the Father except the Son and any one to whom the Son chooses to reveal him.' Jesus is the means whereby the Father is revealed to men. All men must come to Him if they would know God as Father. Mark 13: 32 has a somewhat similar import. It gives an ascending order, and places the Son with the Father above men and angels.

That Jesus knew Himself to be the Son of God in a special way is implied by the temptation narratives. Otherwise the temptations would have had no significance. Perhaps the same might be said about the transfiguration. With this we should place the incident recorded in Luke 2: 42–52. The question of the boy, 'Did you not know that I must be in my Father's house?' shows that even at the age of twelve years Jesus was conscious of His special sonship. The divine voice at the baptism is not then a revelation made to Jesus for the first time. As Vincent Taylor says, 'the words are best understood as an assurance, or confirmation, of this relationship, rather than a disclosure or revelation.'[1]

Again, it may fairly be held that Jesus implied a relation of sonship in at least one of His parables, that of the Labourers in the Vineyard, where we read of 'a beloved son' who is also described as 'the heir' (Mk. 12:6f.). Compare also the statement 'The kingdom of heaven may be compared to a king who gave a marriage feast for his son' (Mt. 22:2). These statements are parabolic, and therefore must not be pressed unduly. But neither should they be overlooked.

The disciples seldom used 'Son of God' (see Mt. 14:33; 16: 16). In view of their avoidance of the term it is somewhat surprising to find the enemies of Jesus using it. The High Priest and his associates asked Him whether He was the Son of God (Mt. 26:63; Mk. 14:61; Lk. 22:70). The Jews told Pilate that He had claimed to be the Son of God (Jn. 19:7), and the mockers at the cross said much the same (Mt. 27:43; *cf.*

[1] In his *Commentary on Mark* (1: 11).

verse 40). The impression made by the whole body of the teaching of Jesus and His attitude to God was evidently such that men felt Him to be claiming a special position for Himself, quite apart from specific words which might be quoted. The general drift of His life and teaching was plain enough.

It remains to ask what we are to make of all this. 'Son of God' could mean much or little. For example, we find the expression in the book of Wisdom, 'For if the righteous man is God's son, he will help him' (2:18). In the light of Luke. 23:47 it is likely that this is the way in which the utterance of the centurion in Matthew 27:54 and Mark 15:39 is to be understood. Then there are passages where the term is applied to Israel as a whole, to individual men, or to angels. But when it is used of Jesus the evidence shows it is not to be taken as meaning that He is Son in the same sense as other men are or might become. He is the Father's 'beloved son' (Mk. 12:6). We come back to the point that while Jesus taught men to know God as Father, He never used any expression which would indicate that He stood in a like relation to God as did they.

Sometimes it is said that 'Son of God' was an accepted Messianic title. This, however, does not seem to be the case. The Jews made little use of the expression, perhaps owing to the anthropomorphic associations it might arouse, and to their reluctance to pronounce the name of God. W. Manson cites evidence to show that in the Targums and the Talmud the expression is largely avoided or explained away.[1] The expression is found in the fourth Book of Ezra and in the Book of Enoch, but it does not appear to be cited elsewhere. Dalman says forthrightly, 'it must be recognized as certain . . . that "Son of God" was not a common Messianic title.'[2]

Thus when Jesus thought of Himself as 'Son of God' (or when other people thought of Him in this way) this was not a conventional allusion to Messiahship. It was a recognition that His Person was such that He could not be described in purely human categories.

[1] *Op. cit.*, pp. 105f.
[2] *Op. cit.*, p. 272.

Forgiver of sin

Jesus offended the religious sensibilities of the men of His day by claiming for Himself divine prerogatives. Thus when a paralysed man, carried by four friends, was lowered through the roof before Him, He astonished everyone by saying to the man, 'My son, your sins are forgiven' (Mk. 2:5). The scribes thought to themselves 'Why does this man speak thus ? It is blasphemy! Who can forgive sins but God alone ?' (verse 7). The reaction of Jesus is interesting and significant. He did not say, 'You are wrong. Men can forgive sins as well as God.' Nor, 'I am not really forgiving this man's sin, but only assuring him that God does so.' He assumed that the scribes were right in thinking of forgiveness as a divine prerogative, and went on from there. He pointed out that it is easy to say, 'Your sins are forgiven'; but it is also easy to say to a paralytic, 'Take up your pallet and walk.' Then He went on: ' "But that you may know that the Son of man has authority on earth to forgive sins" – he said to the paralytic – "I say to you, rise, take up your pallet and go home." And he rose, and immediately took up the pallet and went out before them all' (verses 10–12). In the context Jesus wrought the miracle for the express purpose of demonstrating that He had the power to forgive the man's sins. This vitiates the interpretation that Jesus meant that man can forgive sin,[1] an interpretation which 'reduces the saying to bathos, and indeed to blasphemy'.[2] There is not the slightest reason for separating the power to forgive sin from the power to raise the paralytic. The latter is the evidence for the former (*cf.* Moffatt, 'unless the story is arbitrarily dissected, His right to forgive and His power of dealing with disease are to be taken as co-ordinate elements of His personality'[3]). Men at large can no more forgive sin than make paralytics walk.

Judge of mankind

Another divine function which Jesus claimed for Himself is that

---

[1] Jackson and Lake, *op. cit.*, p. 379.

[2] Fuller, *op. cit.*, p. 99.

[3] *The Theology of the Gospels*, London, 1928, p. 151.

of judging men at the last day. This is clearly expressed in a well-known passage, John 5: 25–29. We find it also in the Sermon on the Mount, where Jesus tells what some will say to Him when they stand before Him, and how He will respond (Mt. 7: 22f.). See also the parable of the Tares (Mt. 13: 24–30, 36–43), and the great judgment scene so graphically depicted in Matthew 25:31–46. The Son of man is the Judge, and the attitude of men to Him the final criterion.

This is an extraordinary claim to make. If we try to imagine anyone else making it we shall perhaps see something of the daring involved. We are so used to reading it in the Gospels that it has ceased to surprise us. But if Jesus was anything less than God it is a claim entirely without foundation. No creature can determine the eternal destiny of his fellow-creatures. But Jesus claimed that His would be the final verdict on all mankind.

The Giver of a new Law

Nothing less is involved in His attitude to the divine Law. At this point we must not be misled by a commonplace of modern criticism, namely, that the Bible contains many errors. Some critics are very free in their handling of the Scriptures. They find some things to be the very word of God, and accept them; but they think of others as the errors of a particular age and culture, and accordingly reject them. There is no equivalent attitude among the Jews of the first century. They regarded every word in the Old Testament as truly the word of God. Not one word, not one syllable, not one letter was to be rejected. As God was the Author of it all the only course open to man was to accept it and obey it. Jesus' attitude to the Law must be understood in the light of agreement as to its divine origin. He laid down authoritive provisions which modified those contained in the Law. In the Sermon on the Mount there is something of a refrain, 'you have heard that it was said to the men of old . . . But I say to you.' Each time He lays down some new provision which is to be observed in place of the old.

It is not that He lacked reverence for the Law. On the contrary He constantly appealed to it as final, and there is not the slightest indication that He wanted men to sit loose to its authority. Things must necessarily happen if foretold in Scripture (Mk. 9:12f., 14:49, etc.). Characteristically He saw the Scriptures as pointing to His own mission (Lk. 4:16ff., etc.). The source of error is ignorance of the Bible (Mt. 22:29). Close examination of the passages in the Sermon on the Mount shows us that when Jesus was modifying the ancient Scriptures His expression involves the use of the emphatic 'I'. He was not saying that any man had authority so to handle the Scriptures, but only that He, being what He was, had this authority. The way He puts it is itself a claim to the very highest place, the claim to issue pronouncements as authoritative as those of God the Father.

It is the same with His attitude to marriage. Although He recognized that there was provision for divorce in the Old Testament He proclaimed the indissolubility of the marriage bond (Mt. 19:6). So with the sabbath. This was established in the Law by a divine command, but Jesus said, 'the Son of man is lord even of the sabbath' (Mk. 2:28. Compare His reference to 'something greater than the temple', Mt. 12:6). There are some who hold that 'Son of man' here means man in general, but it is difficult to justify this. In this passage the word 'man' occurs twice, and, as Moffatt says, 'Had the original Aramaic simply meant "man" in both sentences of Mark, it would have been translated as such uniformly, and, besides, Jesus would not have claimed that man was master of the sabbath which God had instituted.'[1] Unless we reject the saying out of hand we must conclude that it assigns to Jesus a place of pre-eminent authority.

The emphatic 'I'

We noted in an earlier section the use of the emphatic 'I' in the Sermon on the Mount. In Greek the form of the verb is enough to tell whether 'I' or 'you' or 'he' is the subject, and there is no necessity for the personal pronoun to be expressed. If it is used it is to give special emphasis. But Jesus often used it, even when there seems to us no special reason for stress. Take,

[1] *Op. cit.*, p. 152.

37

for example, the invitation to heal the centurion's slave. Jesus did not reply simply, 'I will come', but '*I* will come' (Mt. 8:7). When He sent the disciples on a preaching tour He said, '*I* send you out' (Mt. 10:16). He drew attention to His own Person also when speaking of the significance of His expulsion of demons, 'If it is by the Spirit of God that *I* cast out demons . . .', (Mt. 12:28). This emphatic 'I' is surprisingly frequent.

A similar stress can be obtained without the use of this particular pronoun. Quite often our Lord drew attention to His Person by saying that He 'came' to do this or that. 'I came not to destroy, but to fulfil' (Mt. 5:17, RV); 'the Son of man also came not to be served but to serve, and to give his life as a ransom for many' (Mk. 10:45). There are many such examples. Again and again the form of words Jesus used shows a consciousness of purpose which is foreign to the majority of men. Can you imagine a man today saying, 'I have come to be a policeman' (or whatever it is that he is doing)? His emphatic speech set Him apart from others. He knew that He had a divine destiny, and He used language which marked Him off from mankind as a whole.

Men's deepest needs

'Come to me, all who labour and are heavy laden, and I will give you rest. Take my yoke upon you, and learn from me; for I am gentle and lowly in heart, and you will find rest for your souls. For my yoke is easy, and my burden is light' (Mt. 11:28–30). If there is anything more extraordinary than our coming to take words like these as a matter of course, it is that anyone should ever have uttered them. They are staggering in their implications. They amount to a claim to be able to satisfy the deepest needs of the soul of every man. How much farther than that can anyone go?

And they do not stand alone. The Man who uttered them said also, 'I am the bread of life; he who comes to me shall not hunger, and he who believes in me shall never thirst' (Jn. 6:35). He said that men's eternal destiny hinges on their attitude to Him (Mk. 8:35, 38). At the last meal He had with His followers before He was crucified, He took a cup and said over it,

'This is my blood of the covenant' (Mk. 14:24). This is a claim that His death would be the means of establishing men in a new relationship to God. They would be acceptable before God because of the blood that He would shed. Again, He used expressions which imply the closest possible affinity with God. Receiving Him, He said, means receiving the Father (Mt. 10: 40); despising Him despising the Father (Lk. 10:16); seeing Him seeing the Father (Jn. 14:9).

Much more could be quoted. The Gospels are shot through and through with expressions like these. When we weigh their implications we see how impossible it is to think of Jesus as simply a good man and a moral teacher. We must think of Him as mad, or as an impostor, or as God.[1] For the first two there is no evidence whatever. As we read the Gospels we may wonder whether we are sane, but there can be no doubt about Him. Jesus is the sanest of men. Similarly it is preposterous to think of Him as an impostor. What was His motive? What was He trying to do? What did He gain by it? Are we to think that Christianity which, despite the evil lives of some who have professed it, has yet been the source of so much good, is founded on a deception?

But more than this. Some at least of the claims Jesus made have been tested. In response to His invitation men of all ages and men of all lands have come to Him weary and heavy laden, and they have found rest for their souls. How shall we account for this unless He is indeed divine?

The allegiance Jesus demanded
In the most natural fashion Jesus made the most far-reaching demands on men. He was 'in the last degree exacting without being in the least degree arrogant'.[2] Thus He said, 'If any man would come after me, let him deny himself and take up his cross and follow me. For whoever would save his life will lose it; but whoever loses his life for my sake and the gospel's will

[1] A. M. Hunter quotes 'Rabbi' Duncan, 'Christ either deceived mankind by conscious fraud, or he was himself deluded, or he was divine. There is no getting out of this trilemma' (op. cit., p. 90).
[2] T. W. Manson, op. cit., p. 211.

save it' (Mk. 8:34f.). Great leaders throughout the ages have habitually called on their followers to make sacrifices, even to make the utmost sacrifice. But they have always done so for the sake of the cause. During the war years, Winston Churchill rallied the Empire promising nothing but blood, toil, tears and sweat. But this was not that men might serve Churchill. It was that they might serve their country and Empire.

The difference in the case of Jesus is that He called men to attach themselves not to a cause, but to Himself. And there were no half measures in the devotion He demanded from them. 'If any man comes to me and does not hate his own father and mother and wife and children and brothers and sisters, yes, and even his own life, he cannot be my disciple' (Lk. 14:26; cf. Mt. 10:37). Of a piece with this is His demand that those who would follow Him take up their cross (Mt. 10:38; Mk. 8:34; Lk. 14:27). To us this often sounds sufficiently vague not to be disturbing. But those to whom the words were first spoken had seen men take up a cross. They knew that when a man in their village took up his cross and went off down the road he was going on a one-way journey. He would not be back. Taking up the cross stands for the ultimate in sacrifice. But Jesus called on men to make this sacrifice for His sake.

If Jesus is divine there is no more to be said. We owe to God such allegiance and devotion and love. Our love for God must be so great that all other loves by comparison are but hatred. But how can we offer such devotion to any who is no more than a man? And how can anyone who is simply a man demand such sacrifice?

Conclusion

It is sometimes alleged that the expressions used in the Gospels point us simply to a Sonship of an ethical kind. They give us no justification for thinking of a metaphysical union between Jesus and the Father. He Himself claimed no such thing, and His words ought not to be pressed beyond their natural meaning.

It may readily be conceded that Jesus never gave a theoretical description of His relationship to the Father. It may also be conceded that much of what He said about Himself can be understood in terms of a merely ethical relationship. But much cannot. The evidence is overwhelming that Jesus thought of His Sonship as unique. As Dalman put it, 'Nowhere do we find that Jesus called Himself the Son of God in such a sense as to suggest a merely religious and ethical relationship to God, – a relation which others also actually possessed, or which they were capable of attaining or destined to acquire.'[1] His Sonship was unique.

In any case to stop here is to refuse to face the problem. The problem is this. What explanation can we give of the unique consciousness and the unique character of Jesus ? Granted that He did not claim a metaphysical union with God how can we explain the things He said and the things He did with anything short of such a union ? Do not the facts of the case compel us to think of Him as nothing less than God ?

[1] *Op. cit.*, p. 287.

3   Jesus the man

Greek mythology abounds in stories of gods who walked the earth like men. They looked like men. They acted like men. But at the critical point they would throw aside their disguise and by using their divine power show themselves for what they were. They were never really men, but gods in disguise.

To this day some Christians think of Jesus in much the same way. They picture Him as God, walking among men. He looked like a man. He spoke like a man. He lived like a man. But they do not think of Him as really being a man. They shrink from taking seriously those parts of Scripture which speak of His limitations. In effect they understand Him as God, not man. As the previous chapters have shown, the Gospels make it clear that He was God. But if we are to be faithful to the New Testament we cannot accept the addition, 'not man'. There were some early Christians who said that Jesus was not a man but only seemed to be one. They came to be called 'docetists' (from the Greek word for 'to seem'). But when the church thought about what these men were saying they rejected them as heretics. Christians have always agreed that Jesus must be seen as fully man. To say less is to be a heretic. It may not be easy to combine the thoughts of deity and humanity, but the evidence allows us no alternative.

We know little about Jesus' early life. Such evidence as there is, however, shows a normal growth and development. The first and third Gospels preserve genealogies, which point to human descent. He was born as others are. (The virgin 'birth' is actually a misnomer. It was the conception that was miraculous; we know of nothing abnormal about the birth.) Twice Luke tells us how Jesus grew (Lk. 2:40, 52), and both times we get the impression of a perfectly normal life.

At His first temptation Jesus responded with 'Man shall not live by bread alone' (Mt. 4:4). We usually fasten our attention on the great truth that man needs more than bread. But for our present purpose it is worth noticing that Jesus spoke of Himself as 'man'. Otherwise the words would have had no relevance to His situation. He was subject to all the limitations that beset men in general. He could be weary (Jn. 4:6), hungry (Mt. 21: 18; Lk. 4:2), thirsty (Jn. 19:28). From experience He knew that life in the body can be pleasant and that it can be painful.

But human life means more than the body. Our emotional lives are very important and Jesus had emotions just as other men do. He was joyful (Jn. 15:11), and on occasion sorrowful (Mt. 26:37). He could love (Mk. 10:21) and exercise compassion (Mt. 9:36). It is a human Jesus who was astonished at the faith of the centurion (Lk. 7:9) and at the unbelief of the men of Nazareth (Mk. 6:6). Sometimes He was indignant (Mk. 10:14). Sometimes He was angry and grieved (Mk. 3:5).

There are some striking passages in which Jesus is spoken of as being troubled in one way or another. If He were only God this kind of language would not apply to Him. Take, for example, His behaviour at the tomb of Lazarus. John tells us that He 'groaned in the spirit', employing a very down-to-earth expression, a verb used of horses snorting! Jesus was troubled and wept (Jn. 11:33, 35).

He was troubled also when He faced death. Luke speaks of Him as under constraint until the ordeal was over (Lk. 12:50) and John says that His soul was troubled (Jn. 12:27). In Gethsemane He longed for human companionship and took His three most intimate followers to watch with Him (Mt. 26: 37f.). As He prayed there He was in agony, in such agony indeed that His sweat fell down to the ground like drops of blood (Lk. 22:44). And there is an air of human desolation about the cry from the cross, 'My God, my God, why hast thou forsaken me?' (Mk. 15:34). It is a very human Jesus who undergoes these experiences.[1]

His humanity does not show out simply in times of undue difficulty. It is there all the time. His whole manner of life was genuinely human. As a boy He lived in subjection to Mary and Joseph (Lk. 2:51). As a man He was subject to the State and paid taxes (Mt. 17:24ff.). People called Him 'a glutton and a drunkard' (Mt. 11:19), and the very making of the accusation, wide of the mark though it was, shows that Jesus must have been living a full and enjoyable human life. Henry J. Cadbury, it is true, argues that the contrast with John the Baptist 'is almost certainly overdrawn. Jesus in a sense was probably ascetic'.[2] But it is more than difficult to get such a meaning out of the passage and we should accept the plain sense that Jesus lived an enjoyable life.

Again, He used to ask questions. Now some people ask questions when they already know the answers; for example, schoolteachers. They are not displaying ignorance but testing the knowledge of others. But mostly we ask questions in order to find out something we don't know and it appears to be this kind of question and not the former that Jesus asked. To take an example at random, when He asked the father of the epileptic boy 'How long has he had this?' (Mk. 9:21) the impression we get is that He wanted the information.

Some of His teaching might be adduced here. One of the things that has exercised New Testament scholars has been the frequent use of apocalyptic language in the Gospels, and specifically by Jesus. In earlier days critics ascribed this language to the early church, and discarded it when the authentic teaching of Jesus was being sought. But few nowadays would take such a line. It is recognized that this was part of Jesus' own method. And it is the method of a man of that day and that place. It is evidence that Jesus was a man of Palestine. Scholars often discern kinship with Rabbinic teach-

[1] B. B. Warfield has a long chapter, 'On the Emotional Life of Our Lord' in *The Person and Work of Christ* (Philadelphia, 1950), pp. 93-145.

[2] *The Peril of Modernizing Jesus* (London, 1962), p. 181.

ing and the implications of this should not be overlooked. They show that Jesus was a man of His time, a first-century, Palestinian Jew.

A religious man

Few of us would spontaneously speak of Jesus as 'a religious man'. We mostly think of Him as someone to be worshipped rather than as someone who worshipped. But the Gospels show us that He was regular in His attendance at public worship (Lk. 4:16). Quite a number of incidents are related as having taken place in the synagogue and this points to His habitual attendance. In addition there are references to His private prayer (*e.g.* Mk. 1:35; 6:46; Lk. 3:21, *etc.*). Sometimes He would pray all night (Lk. 6:12) which is eloquent of His sense of need. The prayer in Gethsemane, to which I have already referred, with Jesus' agony and His sweat falling to the ground (Lk. 22:44), shows a depth of feeling in prayer before which we can only stand in awe.

Even His enemies bore their witness to His trust in God (Mt. 27:43). This, of course, is their word, not His, and James Orr found Jesus' own lack of reference to it significant. 'It cannot but be noticed, further, that, while Christ is unceasing in His inculcation of the duty of "faith" on others, He never in a single instance speaks of Himself as having "faith" in God, or "believing" in God. The reason is the obvious one that in Christ "knowledge" in relation to God – pure, immediate, reciprocal, perfect knowledge – takes the place of what is "faith" in us.'[1] This, however, may be too simple. Granted that Jesus lived closer to God than do we, it yet remains that His attitude to God was such that we must use the word 'trust' to describe it. This shines through on every page of the Gospels. As J. Gresham Machen puts it, 'His faith was real religious faith. His relation to His heavenly Father was not merely that of a child to a father; it was that of a man to his God.'[2] This is

[1] *Revelation and Inspiration* (London, 1909), p. 75.
[2] *Christianity and Liberalism* (New York, 1934), pp. 91f. Similarly Loraine Boettner cites B. B. Warfield, 'He exercised faith' (*Studies in Theology* (Grand Rapids, 1947), p. 186).

a most important part of the Gospel picture. We are not to think of a Jesus who moved serenely through this world untroubled by its difficulties and by those times when it seems that everything is against us and the heavens are silent. He knew what it was to trust the Father in the difficult time.

In short, He was a religious man. He practised those acts of worship and communion with God that are the essence of the way of the man of God. In this as in all things He has set us the example we must follow. He lived by faith. His constant trust in the Father shines through the whole of His life.

The limitations of Jesus' knowledge

We must give a more extended discussion to two parts of the evidence for Jesus' manhood, His ignorance and His temptations. These raise a number of important issues and some of the most bitter divisions among Christians over their understanding of the Person of Jesus rest on their different ways of understanding these factors.

We have already noted that Jesus asked questions, and that the most natural way of understanding this is to see Him as wanting to find out the answers. He did not know. This seems to be the right way of reading the Gospels in many places. On one point, the date of His second coming, we are not left in any doubt. Jesus said explicitly that He did not know when this would be (Mk. 13:32). From this alone it is plain that there was some limitation on His knowledge.

This seems necessary if there is to be a real incarnation. It is of the essence of human life that our knowledge is limited and that we must often act on the basis of that imperfect knowledge. The acquisition of knowledge is usually slow and laborious ('much study is a weariness of the flesh', Ec. 12:12). It would not be human life as we know it but something altogether different if we were not limited in this way. Think how different it would be for the student if he knew at the beginning of the year what questions he would face in his examination paper. That he does not is part of being a student.

This enters into the day-by-day living of all of us, whether we are students or not. It is of the very essence of the matter when we are weighing up alternative courses of action that we do not *know* how either will turn out. We gather all the information we can. Perhaps we obtain the opinions of others who have had to make similar decisions in the past and see what resulted from what they did. But in the end we must make our own decision and we must make it on nothing more than our estimate of the probabilities. There is no way of going beyond that. It scarcely seems necessary to labour the point. Ignorance is an inevitable part of the only human life that we know. It compasses us round at every turn. It is a foe against which we wage constant warfare. But the more we know the more we realize that we don't know. Increase of knowledge never delivers us from the necessity of action on the basis of the partially known.

To think of Jesus without thinking of Him as limited in this way is to put Him outside the human race and to make nonsense of the idea of the incarnation. Without intending to do away with any part of the Christian faith some people seem to have such an idea of Jesus. They picture Him as going on a serene way, knowing all the time all the secrets of the universe, and knowing the secret thoughts of everyone about Him and the outcome of every course of action in which He or they were engaging. If this was the way of it then Jesus was not living a human life. Such a life would have lacked a necessary quality of human life, even human life at the highest level. In any case such a view is out of harmony with the Gospels. As we have seen, the evangelists portray for us a Jesus who was genuinely human.

So far, I think, most Christians would agree. But they are not agreed as to the extent of this ignorance. The problem arises because on occasion Jesus did show a most remarkable knowledge of things of which one who was no more than human would presumably have been ignorant. Thus on one occasion He knew the thoughts of His friends (Lk. 9:47) and on another of His enemies (Lk. 6:8, *etc.*). John tells us that He knew the secret experience of Nathanael (Jn. 1:47f.), the past life of the woman of Samaria (Jn. 4:29), and even 'what was in man' (Jn. 2:25).

One solution to this problem is that suggested by E. J. Bicknell, who made a distinction between what he calls Jesus' 'discursive knowledge' and His 'intuitive knowledge'. The former is that gained 'either by the operation of our mind, by processes of reasoning or argument, or else by receiving information from others'. Intuitive knowledge, he thinks, is that gained 'not piecemeal, but by a direct and immediate perception'. Bicknell thinks that Jesus was limited like all other men as regards the former, but not as regards the latter.[1]

The distinction may have its uses but it does not seem to account for all the facts. It does not explain, for example, how Jesus knew the past of the woman of Samaria, nor how He knew that Lazarus was dead (Jn. 11:11-14). It is better to resolve the question in terms of Jesus' mission. He had come to discharge the divine purpose, and such knowledge as was necessary for the discharge of this purpose was given Him. But in all other matters His genuine humanity forbids us to think of Him as in any better position than we are.

That Jesus was ignorant in some matters and that this ignorance arose of necessity from His real humanity, most would agree. But does this mean that He was in error in some things? Many modern scholars unhesitatingly answer 'Yes'. They see Him as just as much a child of His age as we are of ours, and therefore, He must have been wrong in many things. Specifically they see Him as mistaken about the date of the second coming, and about the authorship of the Pentateuch. Scholars of this kind see error as just as much part of humanity as ignorance and they think that Jesus would not be human if He was not wrong in many matters.

But to others it seems crystal clear that ignorance is not the same thing as error. They agree that we must think of Jesus as being ignorant on many matters but that we do not have the same compulsion to think of Him as being in error. For example James Orr could say: 'Ignorance is not error, nor does the one thing necessarily imply the other. That Jesus should

[1] *A Theological Introduction to the Thirty-nine Articles of the Church of England* (London, 1933), pp. 88f.

use the language of His time on things indifferent, where no judgment or pronouncement of His own was involved, is readily understood; that He should be the victim of illusion, or false judgment, on any subject on which He was called to pronounce, is a perilous assertion.'[1] If I understand him aright Orr is saying that Jesus may well have shared the usual ideas of the day about, say, the shape of the earth. But then He made no statement on this topic. Where He did make a statement He knew what He was talking about and was not wrong. Leonard Hodgson makes the important point that to assume that error is a necessary part of human life makes the mistake of measuring Jesus' manhood by ours rather than ours by His.[2]

It should also be borne in mind that there is no real proof that Jesus was wrong in any matter. Many hold that He expected the second coming to take place within the lifetime of the disciples and this is often strongly urged as showing that He was mistaken. But it is met by Jesus' own statement that He did not know when this would take place (Mk. 13:32). Others suggest that He was wrong in His views about the authorship of the Pentateuch and other biblical books and in the events in the life of Jonah. But, no matter how sure some modern scholars are in their own minds about the truth of the matter in all such questions, it is impossible in the nature of the case to produce conclusive proof. Nothing in the available evidence *proves* that Jesus was in error.

There is a tendency today for men to be so convinced of the manhood of Jesus that His Godhead is to all intents and purposes lost sight of. Each age has its own particular insights and ours sees clearly that Jesus was a man. But in stressing His humanity we must be careful not to bring Jesus down to our level in every respect. There is a tendency to see Jesus as nothing more than a typical first-century Jew, wrong in all the ways that such a Jew was wrong, though right in some of His insights into the ways of God. In holding fast to His community with us such a view can surrender His community with God.

Let me say quite plainly that Jesus was a man. Any approach

[1] *Op. cit.*, pp. 105f.
[2] *And Was Made Man* (London, 1933), p. 27.

that obscures or plays down this great truth fails to do justice to the evidence. Nothing must be allowed to obscure the fact that there was a real incarnation. But it must be asserted just as plainly that Jesus was not only a man. He was more. And His limitations must be understood in the light of that 'more'. Admittedly we are faced here with mystery. The point is that the incarnation is unique. We have nothing to compare it with. Finite minds cannot grasp all that is involved in the concept of incarnation, nor can they work out how such a phenomenon could take place. But we must insist that Scripture speaks of a real incarnation. God became man. We must understand the manhood in such a way that the very real Godhead is not ruled out.

The temptations of Jesus

At the beginning of His public ministry Jesus was tempted in the wilderness. At the end He was tempted in Gethsemane. He was tempted on other occasions also as we see from Luke's statement that the devil left Him only 'until an opportune time' (Lk. 4:13).[1] The temptations are important evidence of the true humanity of Jesus, for, as James informs us, 'God cannot be tempted with evil' (Jas. 1:13). The fact that He was subjected to real temptations shows that the incarnation meant the taking of a true manhood.

It is sometimes objected that the temptations of Jesus cannot have been real temptations, since Jesus was sinless. Throughout the centuries Christians have felt that His sinlessness is important and that it must not be taken as more or less fortuitous, the kind of thing that might or might not have occurred, or that it just happened that He did not sin. Such a view would never satisfy the Christian. We cannot take up a position that leaves His sinlessness more or less a matter of chance.

But it is a fallacy to hold that this rules out the possibility of real temptation. To take up such a position is to assume, as

[1] I am not unaware that Hans Conzelmann holds that Luke sees Satan as absent during Jesus' ministry. But I do not think this accords with the facts. See Luke 8:12; 10:18; 11:18; 13:16; 22:3, 31 for evidence that Luke did see Satan as active throughout the ministry.

A. E. Taylor points out, 'that *if* a man does not commit certain transgressions . . . it must be because he never felt the appeal of them.'[1] This is simply not true even in the case of people like ourselves, and we have no reason for affirming it of Jesus. Every moral man daily experiences temptations to which he does not yield. He appreciates the force of them. Otherwise they would not be temptations. But he does not yield to them.

William Temple had some wise words to say on the same subject. Of the paradox that Jesus was genuinely tempted and yet could not yield to the temptation he remarked: 'This is not even a paradox to any one who has seriously considered what is involved in the temptation felt by a man of high character to an act contrary to his character: he is attracted by the wrong course; he has to keep a hold on himself; he knows he is making a real choice; yet (being himself) he could not yield. The effort needed to overcome the temptation is a real effort, but it is also a necessary effort because his character, being such as it is, must so react to the situation.'[2] That Temple is correctly describing what happens to every man of high character from time to time can scarcely be doubted. And if this may be the case even with a moral man, how much more in the case of such a one as Jesus.

It is also to be borne in mind that a man does not have to experience every temptation for him really to be tempted. John McIntyre can refer to St Anselm as observing 'the goodness of a person whose actions are good, not because they are always done in resistance to temptation, but because they flow from an upright character.' He goes on, 'As Professor A. E. Taylor once said: "We have no high regard for the character of the person who has to go through an intense moral struggle

[1] *Asking Them Questions*, ed. Ronald Selby Wright (Oxford, 1942), p. 94.
[2] *Christus Veritas* (London, 1925), p. 217. *Cf.* also D. M. Baillie, 'When we say *non potuit peccare*, we do not mean that He was completely raised above the struggle against sin . . . when we say that He was incapable of sinning, we mean that He was the supreme case of what we can say with limited and relative truth about many a good man' (*God Was in Christ* (London, 1948), pp. 14f.).

with temptation every time he passes a public-house, or sees loose change lying on a friend's desk." In short, the goodness of the character effects rightness and praiseworthiness of actions even when no conflicting inclinations are present to provoke opportunity to sin.'[1] In line with this we may say that Jesus had a positive righteousness such that He probably felt no temptation at all to commit some kinds of sin. But our own experience is enough to show us that that gives no freedom from temptation to other kinds of wrongdoing.

The reality of Jesus' temptations is highlighted by the story of Gethsemane. There we read that He was 'in an agony' and that 'his sweat became like great drops of blood falling down upon the ground' (Lk. 22:44). It makes nonsense of the story to say that there was no real struggle. If words mean anything Jesus really did experience a natural human shrinking from the horror of the cross which He yet knew to be the Father's will. His final 'thy will be done' represents a victory won the hard way, after severe struggle (notice that in Mt. 26:39 He prays that if possible the cup should pass from Him, but in verse 42 the inevitability of the cup is accepted). The story is meaningless unless Jesus wrestled with a real temptation.

It is true that Jesus' experience lacked one element of ours, namely the consciousness of past sin. This gives a peculiar quality to some kinds of temptation. But it does not mean that the man without it does not suffer temptation. After all, it is not unusual for us to experience a 'first' in temptation and in sin, when we find ourselves giving way to something new in the way of temptations. Adam was genuinely tempted, though before that first temptation he had had no experience of sin. We must not make the mistake of taking our imperfect lives as the standard and of regarding Jesus as human only as He conforms to our failures. He is the standard. We find what genuine humanity can be from His perfection rather than from our failures.

We should also bear in mind that, far from sinlessness meaning something less in the way of temptation, human experience suggests that it means more. 'The resistance of

[1] *St Anselm and His Critics* (Edinburgh and London, 1954), p. 148.

temptation may be torture to a good man, whereas a bad man yields easily.'[1] The man who yields to a particular temptation has not felt its full power. He has given in while the temptation has yet something in reserve, so to speak. Only the man who does not yield to a temptation, the man who, as regards that particular temptation, is sinless, knows the full extent of the temptation. Thus Jesus, the sinless One, is the only one who really knows the full extent of temptation's power, and He knows it precisely because He did not yield. If the correct interpretation of 1 Corinthians 10:13 is that there is a correlation between a temptation and the power to endure, then Jesus' temptations must have been of an intensity inconceivable to us.

The certainty of Jesus' temptation might also be a conclusion from the fact that He lived with a body like ours. Bodily life seems necessarily to involve the possibility of temptation. Each bodily appetite carries with it the temptation to misuse it. Thus hunger means that we must eat, but it also means that sometimes we will be tempted to gluttony. The need for rest points to the possibility of laziness. And so we could go on. We cannot see how a body could function without from time to time presenting the possibility of the temptation to indulge our appetites.

With this we should take the fact that in this life wrong means often seem plausible when the end is the right one. The mission of Jesus was such that it could be truly forwarded only by using the right means. But the temptation narrative shows that Jesus felt the temptation to use wrong means for His right purpose. All this reminds us of a statement of R. C. Moberly: 'There was a hypothetical or conceivable selfishness, – the possible imagination of a rebellious self, – not actual indeed, nor actually possible without chaos: yet something to be, by moral strain, controlled and denied; something which made self-denial in the Incarnate, not an empty phrase, but a stupendous act or energy of victorious moral goodness.'[2] If we are to think

[1] H. R. Mackintosh, *The Person of Jesus Christ* (Edinburgh, 1914), p. 403.

[2] *Atonement and Personality* (London, 1932), p. 106.

of Jesus as a good man it is this that we must bear in mind. His sinlessness was not an automatic necessity. It was something attained only by the constant defeat of temptation.

To think of Jesus as going serenely on life's way with never a ripple of real temptation to disturb His calm progress is to empty His moral life of real worth. It reduces Him to the level of a marionette and prevents us from seeing in Him our Example. His sinlessness did not result from some automatic necessity of His nature but from His moment by moment committal of Himself to the Father.[1] He overcame. But it was a real victory, over real temptation.

From all this it is clear that the Gospels speak of a real incarnation. When the Son of God came to earth He did not play at being man. He became man. We may give this expression all the meaning it can bear as D. M. Baillie, for example, has made abundantly clear in his fascinating essay, *God Was in Christ*. The mechanics of the process are hid from us. But the Bible leaves us in no doubt as to the fact. We may be totally unable to explain how the second Person of the Trinity could be exercising His cosmic functions and at the same time be the Babe of Bethlehem. But that does not give us licence to reject that part of the evidence that displeases us.

The facts of the previous chapters point us to the deity of our Lord. Those of this chapter indicate no less clearly His manhood. By this I do not mean that He sometimes acted as God and sometimes as man as though He were a split personality. The Gospels make it abundantly clear that He was one Person and that He lived and acted as a unity. We can divide up the evidence for our own convenience and say, 'This part shows that He was God and that part shows that He was man.' But this must not be understood as though the Godhead and the manhood are separable. However else we understand Him we must think of Him as a unified Person.

[1] *Cf.* the words of William Temple, quoted on p. 23 above.

4 A Prince and a Saviour

'God has made him both Lord and Christ, this Jesus whom you crucified' (Acts 2:36). These words from the first recorded Christian sermon express the emphatic, divine reversal of the judgment men passed on Jesus. They set Him at naught and rejected Him. But God raisd Him from the dead and exalted Him to the highest place of all, so confounding their wicked plans.

The triumph of God rings through the early chapters of Acts. This does not mean that His followers first thought of Jesus as Messiah after the resurrection. As we have seen, His high position was clear during His lifetime. But the resurrection gripped the imagination of those first believers and revolutionized their outlook. 'Not only did it convince the disciples that Jesus was richly and overflowingly alive; it wrote a new chapter in Theology.'[1] Their understanding of God deepened. They learned that the foolishness of God is wiser than men and the weakness of God stronger than men. They were insignificant as the world counts greatness, but they felt a sense of triumph. They were on the side of the mighty God. The breathtaking fact of the resurrection and the invigorating gift of the Holy Spirit combined to drive away the gloom of Good Friday. The believers lived as men possessed by the very Spirit of God.

[1] H. E. W. Turner, *The Life and Person of Jesus Christ* (London, 1951), p. 53.

Men caught up like this in 'the uprush of life' are not systematic theologians. It would be unrealistic to seek from them a formal Christology, or carefully worked-out doctrine of the Person and work of Christ. But it would be just as unrealistic to rob what they say about their Master of its significance for an understanding of His Person. It may well be that we shall have to wait until we come to the theologians of he New Testament for such carefully thought-out statements; but that does not mean that these early affirmations are unimportant. They contain all the raw materials for a very thoroughgoing Christology. As soon as men began to reflect on the significance of the things they were saying such a Christology was bound to emerge.

The manhood of Jesus

First let it be clear that they were in no doubt as to the genuine humanity of the man of Nazareth. They freely used the human name 'Jesus'. They spoke of Him as 'a man attested . . . by God' (Acts 2:22). They said that God was 'with him', that He 'anointed' Him with 'the Holy Spirit' (Acts 10:38). Jesus, they said, 'went about doing good' (*ibid.*). They remembered His words (Acts 20:35). Repeatedly they referred to His sufferings and death (Acts 2:23; 3:15; 4:10, *etc.*). Often the wickedness of those who slew Him is emphasized, but this only highlights their conviction of His very real humanity. There was no divine intervention to blast such evildoers off the face of the earth. Throughout all the early writings it is clear enough that the true manhood was neither overlooked nor minimized.

Divine activity in Jesus

But if the little band had thought in terms of the earthly life only, and confined their thinking of Jesus to His human limitations, they would never have surmounted the tragedy of the crucifixion. That this event had shattered their little world is clear enough from the Gospels. But the action of God altered all that. Again and again it is insisted that the resurrection was due to none less than God Himself (Acts 2:24, 32; 5:30; 10:40; 13:30). It was not a 'natural' event. It was not due to wizardry or magic. It was God's action. The Person of Christ must be seen in the light of this fact.

They looked back to the earthly life of Jesus and saw the miracles as 'signs' from God (Acts 2:22; cf. 10:38). As W. Manson says, 'At the most ancient level of Christian preaching which is known to us the proclamation of Jesus as Messiah was supported primarily by appeal to the "signs" attending his ministry.' This preaching emphasized the miracles as 'acts of God attending Jesus and investing him outwardly and visibly with revelational significance'.[1] If He could reveal God He must partake of the nature of God.

They saw God in the crucifixion. Instead of reasoning that one who died under the curse of heaven could not be the Christ, the early church boldly interpreted the felon's death her Lord had died as taking place 'according to the definite plan and foreknowledge of God' (Acts 2:23). God was in it, too. It was not a crushing disaster. It was God's purposeful action.

Frequently Jesus is seen as the object of prophecy. This is put in general terms (Acts 7:52; 10:43), and with reference to particular events like the crucifixion (Acts 3:18 and often) or the resurrection (Acts 2:25-31). God had glorified Jesus (Acts 3:13). God had exalted Him to His own right hand (Acts 2:33; 1 Pet. 3:22). God had made Him both Lord and Christ (Acts 2:36). God had chosen Him to be the Judge of all men, living and dead alike (Acts 10:42; 17:31).

Words could hardly give more emphatic expression to the thought that the Father had borne witness to the Son. The early believers saw God in every aspect of the work of Jesus, past, present, and future. His stature was nothing less than divine.

The Lord

Something of the place the early believers assigned to Jesus is to be discerned from a study of the names they gave Him. First in importance here is 'Lord'. This word was used in more ways than one. Minus the article the Greek term was an ordinary

[1] *Jesus the Messiah* (London, 1944), p. 33.

form of polite address, much like our 'Sir'. It is used in this fashion by the son who said, 'I go, sir' (Mt. 21:30), and the Greeks who said to Philip, 'Sir, we wish to see Jesus' (Jn. 12:21). It could be used by students addressing their teacher, like the Hebrew equivalent, 'Rabbi'. With the article it could denote a man in an important position, like the master of slaves (Lk. 12:45ff.), or even the Roman Emperor (Acts 25:26). It was thus a word which could mean much or little. But there were some specifically religious uses of the term, and from our point of view these are most important.

Here we must bear in mind Deissmann's comment, ' "Lord" is a term instinct with Oriental feeling; the kings of the East have from time immemorial been "lords," and their subjects nothing better than slaves.'[1] Even if we accept the kindlier view of W. Robertson Smith that the word really represents 'a refinement of Semitic politeness', and that when a man speaks of his god as 'lord' and himself as 'servant', he means that he is 'specially devoted to his service and worship',[2] it is still a term which gives strong expression to the gulf between man and God. It is in keeping with this emphasis on the transcendence of God that 'Lord' was used in the Greek translation of the Old Testament to render the divine name, Jehovah. At the same time it must be borne in mind that this is in Greek translation. There is little evidence that the Aramaic equivalent, *Mar*, was used in this way. Yet at the very least we must say that Greek-speaking Christian Jews applied to Jesus the title characteristically employed of Jehovah in their sacred Scriptures. H. E. W. Turner thinks that this could represent 'the simplest possible way of affirming that centrally and essentially, in the depths of His Being, Jesus stood on the side of God rather than on that of creatures'.[3]

It was in Greek that the word 'Lord' had its principal religious use. It was the common word used in the East by worshippers when they referred to their god. It was the 'dis-

---

[1] *Light from the Ancient East* (London, 1927), p. 350.
[2] *The Religion of the Semites* (London, 1927), pp. 68f.
[3] *Jesus, Master and Lord* (London, 1953), p. 228.

tinctively honourable title of the divine centre of a cult'.[1] Especially was it used in this way of the Roman Emperors when they came to be revered as divine. Deissmann cites a large volume of evidence to show that this was the case, particularly in the East.[2] Indeed, Dalman thinks it is this use which gives us the clue to the Christian use of the term: 'When the Christians called Jesus *ho kurios*, they will have meant that He is the true "divine Lord," in opposition to the "God and Lord" on the imperial throne of Rome.'[3]

That to some extent in Jewish circles, and very obviously in Greek circles, the word denoted one who was divine is clear enough. It remains to ask whether it was the Jewish-Christian church or the Gentile church which first came to think of Jesus in this way. Bousset, in his books *Kyrios Christos* and *Jesus der Herr*, argued strongly that the title was first used by Gentile Christians.[4] It may readily be conceded that in the Gospels Jesus is not often referred to as 'the Lord'.[5] But when we come to Acts it is a different matter. The earliest speeches refer to Jesus in this way (*e.g.* Acts 2:36), and these speeches are usually taken as being reliable. F. F. Bruce examines them carefully, and concludes that Luke is summarizing, but faithfully. Luke 'would naturally introduce more or less of his own style; but in point of fact it frequently seems to be less, not more.' Professor Bruce concludes that there is 'good ground, in my judgment, for believing these speeches to be, not inventions of the historian, but condensed accounts of speeches actually made, and therefore valuable and independent sources of the

[1] Jackson and Lake, *The Beginnings of Christianity*, II (London, 1920), p. 411.

[2] *Op. cit.*, pp. 349ff.

[3] *The Words of Jesus* (Edinburgh, 1902), p. 330.

[4] There is a very useful summary of Bousset's views in Appended Note I to A. E. J. Rawlinson's *The New Testament Doctrine of the Christ* (London, 1926).

[5] Yet, even so, this did occur. Compare J. Y. Campbell, 'There seems no good reason to doubt that even during his lifetime his own Disciples called Jesus "Master and Lord" (John 13. 13).' *A Theological Word Book of the Bible*, ed. Alan Richardson (London, q950) p. 131.

history and theology of the primitive Church'.[1] There is every reason then for holding that the first Christians freely spoke of Jesus as 'Lord'.

There is an interesting piece of evidence from I Corinthians, namely, the *Maranatha* of I Corinthians 16:22 (see RSV margin). This is a piece of Aramaic, and thus it must have come from the Jewish and not the Gentile Church. It is usually taken as meaning 'Our Lord, come!' and, while there may be some dispute as to its exact meaning (it might be 'Our Lord has come' or even 'Our Lord comes'), there is no disputing the fact that here is a piece of Aramaic which applies the term 'Lord' to Jesus, and that in a sense 'implying religious devotion'.[2]

On the whole, then, it seems that the title 'Lord' was first applied to Jesus by the Jewish church, and that for them it had divine overtones. Then, as the faith spread to Gentile areas, the new converts found in this term a word which gave satisfying expression to the idea that Jesus was the divine Lord. Succinctly it gave Him the highest place of all. Its associations with the cultus of more than one god made it a very suitable word to express the deity of Him to whom it was applied. Thus it came into widespread use in the Gentile church.

His other titles

The first Christians addressed Jesus by a bewildering assortment of other titles. We have already discussed 'Christ' in chapter two. Here we need add only that it was used so regularly that it developed into a proper name. It was used by itself, and in various combinations such as 'Jesus Christ' and 'the Lord Jesus Christ'. When Jewish lips used the word of the risen and ascended Jesus it carried all the significance the title was capable of bearing. Which is to say that it made of Jesus a divine Person.

He was also called the 'Holy One' (Acts 2:27; 3:14), the 'Righteous One' (Acts 3:14; 7:52; 22:14), 'the Author of life'

[1] *The Speeches in the Acts* (London, 1942), p. 27. A. M. Hunter says, 'there is no need to reiterate that these speeches presume early tradition and may be taken to reflect primitive Christian thought about Jesus'. *The Unity of the New Testament* (London, 1944), pp. 34f.

[2] A. E. J. Rawlinson, *op. cit.*, p. 235.

(Acts 3:15), 'the stone' (Acts 4:11; I Pet. 2:4ff.), 'thy holy servant' (Acts 4:27, 30), 'a Prince and a Saviour' (Acts 5:31, AV), the prophet foretold by Moses (Acts 3:22f.; *cf.* 7:37), 'the Son of man' (Acts 7:56), 'the Son of God' (Acts 9:20), 'a Saviour' (Acts 13:23), 'another king, Jesus' (Acts 17:7), 'the Lord of glory' (Jas. 2:1), 'the Shepherd and Guardian of your souls' (I Pet. 2:25), 'the chief Shepherd' (I Pet. 5:4), 'the Judge of the living and the dead' (Acts 10:42), the 'lamb without blemish or spot' (I Pet. 1:19; His sinlessness is affirmed also in 2:22).

It is obvious that these first Christians were men who had had a deep saving experience of Jesus. Out of the depths of this experience they seized on every title that would help to convey anything of His immense significance for them. These names do not represent a systematic classification of Jesus' nature and attributes. They are the artless outpouring of men's deep gratitude as they contemplate Him who has done everything for them. Some of these names soon ceased to be used. They were not adequate for the needs of the church, and thus tended to drop out of the Christian vocabulary. But their occurrence, even only once or twice, helps us to see the large place Jesus occupied in the thoughts of those who used them. The complete inadequacy of language to utter even a fraction of His significance led them to make use of any and every term that would serve their purpose.

It will not be possible to examine all these titles in the space at our disposal. Some of them are obvious enough, even when approached from a background very different from that of the first Christians. But a brief comment will be in order on one or two.

'The Author of life' or 'Author' brings a combination of ideas. The Greek *archēgos* comes from a root connected with beginning. The thought may be one who is first in point of time (as Moffatt's translation 'Pioneer'), or who is first in importance ('Prince', as in the AV), or who is the source ('Author'). It is likely that in its New Testament occurrences the name 'suggests the dual idea of One who is the source of faith, deliverance, and life, and is at the same time the path-breaker who has once opened the way to others.'[1] Jesus went first along the way Himself, but He also brings His people there.

The 'stone' is a reference to the prophecies of Psalm 118: 22f. and Isaiah 28:16. It brings together the thoughts of the rejection by men of that which, nevertheless, is of great intrinsic worth, and that of the stone occupying a decisive place in the building. Interpretations vary as to whether the 'cornerstone' of 1 Peter 2:6 was in the foundation or at the top of the building. But they agree that it is that stone which determines all the rest.

The 'holy servant' makes use of a term which may mean either 'son' or 'slave'. It is the word used of the Suffering Servant of Isaiah 53, and there can be no reasonable doubt but that the use of the term in the early chapters of Acts points us to this prophecy. The term expresses the vicarious suffering of Him who bore it, and was a continual reminder to believers of the lowliness of their Lord, and of the great love He showed in bringing them salvation.

The prophet foretold by Moses (the reference is to Deuteronomy 18:15f.) does not loom large in Jewish writings. It was not a commonly accepted Messianic title. The Samaritans seem to have made more use of it than did the Jews.[2] Moses was not regarded simply as one of the company of prophets. He was of altogether exceptional stature. God spoke to him face to face. His words had divine authority. Through him the Law was given. He could be thought of as the founder of the Jewish nation. The 'prophet . . . like me' of whom he speaks was accordingly an outstanding figure. The Christian use of this term as one of the titles of Jesus does two things at least. It draws attention to the prophetic aspect of His ministry. And it indicates that Jesus far surpasses the prophets.

These early Christians had come to know Christ and to know salvation through Him. Out of the certainty that He had met their souls' deep needs they spoke of Him, ransacking their vocabulary to find words which would express some small

[1] Vincent Taylor, *The Names of Jesus* (London, 1953), p. 91.
[2] See, for example, Jackson and Lake, *op. cit.*, pp. 404, 406. It is not likely, as these writers suggest, that the Christian use was influenced by the Samaritan.

fraction of all that they owed to Him and thought of Him. He had done for them what no mere man could have done, and in this galaxy of titles they do but acknowledge the fact.

His saving activity

'God, having raised up his servant, sent him to you first, to bless you in turning every one of you from your wickedness' (Acts 3:26). In these words Peter directs men's minds to the fact that Jesus' mission was to turn men away from sin. He was sent by God for this very purpose. But to deal adequately with sin a very special Person is needed, and thus in this same verse Peter reminds us that the One who was to do this stood in a special relationship to God. Although this is not always stressed, it is always implied in the many statements about Christ's saving work. God exalted Him 'to give repentance to Israel and forgiveness of sins' (Acts 5:31), 'every one who believes in him receives forgiveness of sins through his name' (Acts 10:43), 'through this man forgiveness of sins is proclaimed to you, and by him every one that believes is freed from everything from which you could not be freed by the law of Moses' (Acts 13:38f.), 'we shall be saved through the grace of the Lord Jesus' (Acts 15:11).

There are other statements to the same effect, but it seems hardly necessary to go on. No-one who is familiar with the New Testament writings will doubt that saving significance is invariably ascribed to Jesus from the very earliest times.

Jesus does more than provide for the forgiveness of men's sins. The infant church was first galvanized into activity by the sending of the Holy Spirit. This was prophesied by Jesus (Acts 1:5), and when it took place it was interpreted as the result of the action of Jesus (Acts 2:33). The Spirit can be spoken of as 'the Spirit of Jesus' (so the best manuscripts in Acts 16:7). This is probably also the meaning of 'the Spirit of the Lord' in Acts 5:9; 8:39. The Spirit is 'the Spirit of Christ' (1 Pet. 1:11). The gift of the Spirit is associated with baptism in the name of Jesus (Acts 2:38; cf. also 19:5f.). Jesus sent Ananias to Saul in order that he might receive sight and be filled with the Holy Spirit (Acts 9:17).

The picture then that we get from all this is of Jesus as the One who saved men from their sins, and who then sent His Spirit to them. Their initial deliverance from sin is ascribed to Him, and their continuing life in the power of the Spirit is also due to Him.

Jesus will come again in the completion of His work. This was prophesied in the very moment of His ascension (Acts 1: 11). Peter told the men at the Gate Beautiful of the 'times of refreshing' that will come when the Father sends Jesus Christ (Acts 3:19f.). The theme recurs in the Epistle of James (5:7f.) and in that of Peter (1 Pet. 1:7, 13; 4:13; 5:4). The consummation of all things in the return of the Lord from heaven is looked for throughout the New Testament.

Men's attitude to Jesus

It is in keeping with all this that the attitude that men have, or should have, to Jesus is the attitude that they have, or should have, to God. Thus James begins his Letter with 'James, a servant of God and of the Lord Jesus Christ' (1:1). There is no argument. There is no reasoned theological statement. But easily and naturally James puts Jesus alongside God the Father, and there is no sense of incongruity.

The characteristic attitude to Jesus is that of faith (Acts 5:14; 9:42; 10:43; 11:17, etc.), and there are other expressions like 'faith toward our Lord Jesus Christ' (Acts 20:21, AV), 'faith in Christ Jesus' (Acts 24:24), or 'the faith of our Lord Jesus Christ' (Jas. 2:1). This kind of thing goes beyond the trust a man might legitimately have in his fellow, and is the authentic religious attitude of a man to his God.

In Acts 3:16 we read of 'faith in his name' and this will serve to introduce us to the large place accorded to 'the name' of Jesus. To modern Western men a name is a mere appellative; but to men of ancient times it stood for the whole person. They paid especial reverence to the name of God. The Jews would not pronounce this name, but used some reverential periphrasis for it. One such alternative was simply 'the Name'. It is against such a background that we must see the use of the name of Jesus.

In Acts 'the name' is almost invariably that of Jesus. Men were baptized in this name (Acts 2:38; 8:16, *etc.*). Men were healed in this name (Acts 3:6, 16; 4:10, 30, *etc.*). Even 'some of the itinerant Jewish exorcists' knew that the name of Jesus was used in exorcism (Acts 19:13ff.). Salvation is associated with His name (Acts 10:43; 22:16), and with this name only (Acts 4:12). Men receive forgiveness 'through his name' (Acts 10:43). So it is that men 'call upon' this name (Acts 2:21; 9:14, 21). Men might speak in the name (Acts 4:17f.), speak boldly in it (Acts 9:27, 29), teach in it (Acts 4:18; 5:28), or preach concerning it (Acts 8:12). Paul was to 'carry' the name before Gentiles and kings and the children of Israel (Acts 9:15), and to suffer for it (Acts 9:16). Apostles rejoiced 'that they were counted worthy to suffer shame for his name' (Acts 5:41). Barnabas and Paul 'have hazarded their lives for the name of our Lord Jesus Christ' (Acts 15:26). Paul declared himself ready to die for the name (Acts 21:13). Contrariwise the persecutions of the church in which he had once engaged could be described as doing things 'opposing the name' (Acts 26:9). Small wonder that the name of Jesus 'was extolled' (Acts 19:17), and that believers could speak of 'the honourable name' by which they were called (Jas. 2:7). When they became known as 'Christians' (Acts 11:26) they were associated with this name. The bearer of such a name was clearly regarded as no less than divine.

Nothing more graphically illustrates the high place accorded to Jesus than the fact that prayer was offered to Him. It seems probable that He is the 'Lord' who is addressed in such places as Acts 1:24; 8:24; 10:14, and this is beyond dispute in Acts 22:19, as also in the prayer of Stephen (Acts 7:59, 60). Men address their prayers to God. Those who prayed to Jesus obviously had a very high view of His Person.

In keeping with this the early church looked to Jesus to perform miracles through them, as we saw in the section on the 'name' of Jesus (so also Acts 14:3). The early believers understood that their task was to bear witness to Jesus (Acts 1:8; 10:39, 41), and to preach Him (Acts 8:5; 9:20, *etc.*). They thought of their 'behaviour' as being 'in' Him (1 Pet. 3:16).

Perhaps we should see the high point of all this in the way in which Old Testament passages which refer to Jehovah are applied to Jesus. This is done in Acts 2:21, where Joel 2:32 is used of Him. We see it again in 1 Peter 3:15, which should be taken as RV, 'sanctify in your hearts Christ as Lord,' and is clearly an application of Isaiah 8:13, 'Sanctify the Lord of hosts himself.' In similar fashion 1 Peter 2:3 may well be an application of the words of Psalm 34:8. This is a phenomenon common in the New Testament, and, when we consider how jealously the position of Jehovah was safeguarded by those who worshipped Him, we are able to see something of the high place they accorded Christ.

We conclude this section by drawing attention to Acts 20:28, which refers to 'the church of God, which he hath purchased with his own blood' (AV). It may be, as Bruce maintains, that this should be understood in the sense 'the blood of His own One'[1] (cf. RSV), but even so the verse must be interpreted along the lines suggested by Rackham, 'The real solution is to be found in the doctrine of the Trinity, which is here implicit.'[2]

Our conclusion from all this is that it is impossible to accept what the early believers said about Jesus and still stop short of ascribing deity to Him. It may be that part of the evidence can be understood without this, but not all. Christians knew that they had been saved, in all the fullness that that word signifies, in and by Christ. They knew that one who is only a man cannot save his fellows in this way. Thus they removed Jesus from the merely human level in all their thinking. There is no formal definition of His deity, but the multiplicity of their statements about Him make sense only if we think of Him as one with God. Sometimes they employ categories previously used by Jesus. Sometimes they do not. There is a freshness, a spontaneity about their utterances. The important point is that, while they put it in their own way, and do not slavishly repeat the words of Jesus, what they say implies the same high view of His Person. He claimed a special relationship to the Father. In their own way they enthusiastically agree.

[1] The Acts of the Apostles[2] (London, 1952), in loc.
[2] The Acts of the Apostles (London, 1909), in loc.

5 The Lord of glory

In the first century it was the custom in letter-writing to begin
with some pious expresion. 'Gaius to Amplias, greeting. May
the gods preserve you' is the usual kind of thing. This was just
as much a part of a first-century letter as our 'Dear So-and-so'
at the beginning, and 'Yours faithfully' or the like at the end
(even though we may be addressing our worst enemy, and be
not at all faithful in what we write!). The early Christians, of
course, used the conventional form, though they did give it a
twist or two of their own. The interesting thing for our present
purpose is that when Paul was writing a letter it was his habit
to associate the Lord Jesus with the Father in his opening prayer.
'Grace to you and peace from God our Father and the Lord
Jesus Christ' (Rom. 1: 7), he wrote to the Christians at Rome,
and a similar expression is found at the head of every one of his
letters that has been preserved.

This is very revealing. It shows us that Paul held the highest
possible view of the Person of Christ. In the first place, only on
this basis could he have bracketed the Son with the Father. In
the second, he looks to Christ as the source of that grace and
peace which he longs to be made available to his correspon-
dents, wherever they might be.

Another little habit of the great apostle is to interject some
short prayer into the body of a letter. Such prayers are frequent.
On occasion he addresses them to both Father and Son, and
puts his verb in the singular (*e.g.* 1 Thes. 3:11; 2 Thes. 2:16f.).
This is not formal theological definition, but it shows us plainly

enough that Paul thought of Christ as in some sense one with the Father. It is in line with this that he can describe God as 'the God and Father of our Lord Jesus Christ', or some similar phrase (Rom. 15:6; 2 Cor. 1:3; 11:31, *etc.*). We know God the Father in His real character only because Jesus has revealed Him. It is as He is known in Jesus that He is known at all.

Paul is so much in the habit of thinking of the Father and the Son as intimately related that he ascribes many gifts and graces indifferently to either. Thus he can speak of the gospel as the gospel of God (Rom. 1:1), and a few verses later as the gospel of Christ (Rom. 1:16). The two are so close that it doesn't matter which name is used. Nor is this an isolated instance. Forgiveness is from God (Col. 2:13), or from Christ (Col. 3:13), or from God for Christ's sake (Eph. 4:32). Revelation is from Jesus Christ (Gal. 1:12), and it is from the Father (Gal. 1:16). Very significant is the fact that this way of speaking is applied to the church (Gal. 1:13; Rom. 16:16), the Spirit (1 Cor. 2:11; Rom. 8:9), and the Kingdom (Rom. 14:17; Col. 1:13).

If it is true that Paul does not make any marked difference between the Father and the Son when he is thinking of great realities like the Spirit and the Kingdom, and when his thought concerns blessings, it is also true that he has both Persons in mind when the darker matters of judgment are to the fore. He tells us that one day we shall stand before the judgment seat of God (Rom. 14:10–12), but he can also refer to the judgment seat of Christ (2 Cor. 5:10). The Old Testament jealously guards the prerogative of deity, and assures us that vengeance belongs only to God (Dt. 32:35), but Paul has no doubts about the fact that vengeance will be executed by the Lord Jesus (2 Thes. 1:7f.). Again in the Old Testament the great day at the end of the world when judgment would be effected is the 'day of the Lord' (*cf.* Rom. 2:16). Paul speaks boldly of 'the day of our Lord Jesus Christ' (1 Cor. 1:8). Could anything more strikingly demonstrate the place accorded Christ than the spectacle of this convinced Jewish monotheist so freely ascribing divine functions to Him? It might be possible to maintain that one or two expressions such as these are casual, and that no great stress should be placed upon them. But the cumulative force of so many is impressive (and there are many others not cited). Paul habitually associates the Lord Jesus so closely with the Father, that he can ascribe functions to either of Them indifferently. Anyone who has worked closely on the Pauline writings will know that passages are frequent in which there is no great distinction made between Them.

The manhood of our Lord

It is not that Paul is unmindful of the Lord's genuine humanity. He speaks of Him as 'born of woman' (Gal. 4: 4) and again as 'descended from David according to the flesh' (Rom. 1: 3). On other occasions he refers to the 'flesh' of Jesus, as when he says that He was sent 'in the likeness of sinful flesh', and that He condemned sin 'in the flesh' (Rom. 8:3). When he refers to knowing Christ 'after the flesh' (2 Cor. 5: 16, AV) he may even mean that he has seen Jesus in the days of His ministry. But whether that is so or not it is obvious enough from these references that Paul knows that Jesus had a real human body, and that He was a real man.

Paul does not refer to a great number of events in the life of Jesus. He does refer to the institution of the holy communion (1 Cor. 11: 23ff.) and, of course, he often speaks of the sufferings and death of Christ. Paul made the cross the centre of his theology so there can be no doubt as to his interest in it. Sometimes he refers to qualities that Jesus displayed in His earthly life, such as meekness and gentleness (2 Cor. 10:1). Or again, he will refer to His poverty (2 Cor. 8:9), or to His weakness (2 Cor. 13:4).

It would not be true to say that the earthly life of Jesus was a major interest for St Paul. He does not make incidents from it the basis of his instruction. Nor does he commonly refer to the teaching of our Lord, although examples do occur (*e.g.* 1 Cor. 7:10; 9:14). But as we read his Letters it is plain enough that he did know quite a lot about the life of Christ. He recognized that He was fully a man.

The names of Jesus

But He was more than a man. Consider the implications of the titles Paul uses of Him. He uses 'Christ' often; in fact 379 times as against 150 times in all the rest of the New Testament. It is clear that Paul uses this name much more than any other New Testament writer. In fact it is due to him that Christians have the common habit of using 'Christ' as a proper name. Paul may be using the title in this way because his letters were usually written to Gentiles for whom a title like 'the Christ' would not have much meaning. But if 'the Christ' meant little to Gentiles, 'the Lord' meant much. Paul uses 'the Lord' with great frequency and effect. He could, and did, employ it in its fullest sense of the divine Object of worship. But whereas for the Gentile nations in general there were 'many "gods" and many "lords" ', for Paul there could be but 'one Lord, Jesus Christ, through whom are all things' (1 Cor. 8:6; cf. Eph. 4: 5). His constant use of this term was inevitable for, as J. Gresham Machen points out,[1] it was the only term open to him if he wished to refer to Jesus as God in a way which distinguished Him from the Father. 'Our Lord Jesus Christ' is an expression pregnant with meaning. 'Everything a man can feel towards God comes in this name to utterance.'[2]

But Paul does not content himself with repeating the names and titles others had used before him. His was an active and fertile mind, and his Christian experience was deep. His whole life had been transformed by what Christ had done for him. Small wonder then, that his magnificent powers, focused on the one Object of his adoration, illuminated by the Holy Spirit of God, should produce new insights into the wonder of the Person of Paul's divine Lord.

Sometimes Paul is thinking of Christ's pre-eminence, and then he may call Christ the Head over His church (Eph. 4:15; 5:23; Col. 1:18; 2:19), a metaphor which also brings out the unity between the Lord and the Lord's people. Or he may refer to 'the first-born among many brethren' (Rom. 8:29), 'the first-born from the dead' (Col. 1:18), or 'the first-born of all creation' (Col. 1:15). The first two of these remind us that

[1] *The Origin of Paul's Religion* (Grand Rapids, 1947), p. 307.
[2] J. Weiss, cited in C. Anderson Scott, *Christianity According to St Paul* (Cambridge, 1927), p. 254.

Christ underwent experiences Himself in order that He might bring others safely through them. Believers may face death unafraid, because Jesus underwent death for them. He has removed its terrors. Some have misunderstood the third passage by pressing 'creation' to mean that Jesus was a created being, even though the first of such. This, however, is not the meaning. The context clearly excludes any thought that Christ might be a creature. Paul's point is that Christ stands to every creature in the relation of the first-born to his father's property, *i.e.* He is the heir. The word combines the ideas of primacy and sovereignty.

The same passage refers to Him as the 'beginning' (Col. 1:18). This word, too, combines two meanings, that of priority in time, and that of source or origin. Christ came before the church, and He was the source of the church. Through Him it had its being. The same passage tell us that 'in him all the fulness of God was pleased to dwell'. This probably refers to teaching of a gnostic type. Some of the gnostics thought that there were many divine beings, each with his own particular nature and functions. Together they made up the fullness. But Paul will have none of this. He brooks no rival to his beloved Lord. In Christ dwells *all* the fullness.

Sometimes Paul thinks of Jesus in terms of glory. He sees 'the light of the knowledge of the glory of God in the face of Christ' (2 Cor. 4:6). Christ is 'the Lord of glory' (1 Cor. 2:8). The 'glory' may well point us to the very presence of God, as it does in Old Testament passages like Exodus 24:16. More than one scholar has seen in these references the most far-reaching of all the titles that Paul uses of Christ. J. Weiss says that 'the Lord of glory' is 'perhaps the loftiest description of Him to be found in S. Paul'.[1] C. Anderson Scott reminds us that in the Book of Enoch this very expression is frequently used of the Almighty Himself.[2]

There are depths that the casual English reader might not expect in such a description of Jesus as 'the power of God and the wisdom of God' (1 Cor. 1:24). Among the Jews there was

[1] Cited in *Cambridge Greek Testament* on 1 Cor. 2:8.
[2] *Op. cit.*, p. 276.

a superstitious fear of using the name of God. Instead men employed terms like 'the Holy One', 'the Blessed', *etc.* One recognized term was 'the Power'. While Paul is not employing this use exactly (for he adds 'of God'), yet he is associating Christ very closely with the divine Name. The same is true of 'the wisdom of God', for this was commonly used of God's revelation to men (see Pr. 8:22ff.). Outside the Bible the idea is found in books like Ecclesiasticus and the Wisdom of Solomon. W. D. Davies has shown the importance of this concept within Judaism,[1] and makes it very clear that Paul's use of it implies a very high view of the Person of Christ indeed.

Sometimes Paul speaks of Jesus as 'the likeness of God' (2 Cor. 4:4), or 'the image of the invisible God' (Col. 1:15). 'Image' and 'likeness' are the same word in the Greek: *eikōn*. This striking term emphasizes that it is in Jesus that we see what God is like. Some have felt that if He is the 'image' of God, then He cannot be God, for the image and the object of which it is the reflection are not the same. Indeed some would go so far as to say that there is a qualitative difference between the two. But this is to push the metaphor too far. The most that we can allow is that it indicates that the Son is not identical with the Father. The Greek term certainly denotes likeness and not unlikeness. It conveys the thought that Christ represents God, that He shows forth God. When we see Him we see God. Rawlinson says that in this concept Paul 'has approximated with singular closeness to precisely that idea of a co-essential yet derivative Godhead which for later Church orthodoxy was expressed by the doctrine of the eternal generation of the Son'.[2]

Once Paul makes use of the very lovely title, 'the Lord of peace' (2 Thes. 3:16). With us 'peace' is a negative concept. It is the absence of war or strife. But this was not the case among the Jewish-speaking and Jewish-thinking people of antiquity. For them 'peace' was connected with the idea of wholeness. The man who had peace was the man whose life was rounded off, and who was prosperous in the whole range of living. Most important of all, this included a right relationship with God.

---

[1] *Paul and Rabbinic Judaism* (London, 1948), pp. 147-176.
[2] *The New Testament Doctrine of the Christ* (London, 1926), p. 132.

When Jesus is thought of as 'the Lord of peace', then the idea is that He is the source of that full and perfect peace which means the prosperity of the whole man. 'The peace of God, which passes all understanding' is something that comes from Him.

There are many more titles of Jesus. If we were to attempt to be exhaustive in this aspect of Paul's writings we would need a whole book. But this selection is sufficient to demonstrate that from a study of the names and titles that Paul applies to Jesus much can be learned of his view of the Lord. One who could fulfil all that is involved in all these titles must be a very extraordinary Being. Or to put it the other way round, if Jesus is such that all these titles and more are needed to give expression to some small fraction of His significance, then that significance must be very great indeed.

He emptied Himself

Perhaps here we should notice the celebrated passage (Phil. 2: 5ff.) which speaks of Jesus as 'in the form of God', affirms that He 'did not count equality with God a thing to be grasped', and proceeds to speak of His 'emptying' Himself (verse 7), and of His subsequent exaltation. The word *morphē*, 'form', denotes, as Lightfoot long ago showed, the essential characteristics (as contrasted with those which are merely incidental and changeable). Christ has the essential characteristics of God. The word *harpagmos*, which AV renders 'robbery', is more likely in this context to have its secondary meaning, 'that which is highly prized'. The meaning of the expression is thus,'*Though* He pre-existed in the form of God, *yet* He did not look upon equality with God as a prize which must not slip from His grasp, *but* He emptied Himself.'[1]

Having asserted Christ's essential deity Paul goes on to say that the Lord 'emptied himself, taking the form of a servant' (verse 7). Once again the word for 'form' is that for the essential characteristics. Christ's humanity was genuine. There was no make-believe about it. A real incarnation took place. Paul takes this thought right through to its conclusion in the death on the

[1] J. B. Lightfoot, *in loc.*

cross. It is only this which shows the full extent to which He 'humbled himself'.

The consequence of all this is the stamp of divine approval set upon it by the exaltation. Christ is given the ineffable name, that 'name which is above every name'. All things in every place bow to this name, and confess the Lordship of Jesus Christ. This can mean nothing less than the paying of divine honours to Him. The thrust of the passage is that Jesus, though He stooped so low, was yet so high that He must be thought of as one with the Father.

Some modern theologians have interpreted all this to mean that the incarnation was the laying aside by Jesus of His divine attributes. The kenotic theory (to give it its technical name: the word is derived from *kenōsis*, meaning 'emptying'), holds that the Man of Nazareth was a man and nothing more during the time of His life. Before and after this He was God, but during the incarnation His deity was laid aside. Such views hold attractions for many people today. They enable them at one and the same time to treat the life of Jesus as an entirely human phenomenon, and to retain a faith in His full deity. But there seem to be fatal objections to it.

In the first place kenotic views overlook a good deal of the evidence which we considered in the chapters on the Gospels.[1] The Jesus who appears before us there is *not* in point of fact simply a man. He is man, but He is more. Secondly, they do not square with the consistent New Testament idea that an incarnation took place. They give us, not a picture of God becoming man, but of a series of changes, with God turning into a man, and then turning back into God. As D. M. Baillie says: 'If taken in all its implications, that seems more like a pagan story of metamorphosis than like the Christian doctrine of Incarnaion, which has always found in the life of Jesus on earth God and man in simultaneous union – the Godhead "veiled in flesh" but not *changed into* humanity.'[2] Thirdly, the change of the man Jesus back into God after His time on earth seems to imply that the taking of humanity was a temporary incident. This would

[1] See pp. 9-54.
[2] *God Was in Christ* (London, 1948), pp. 96f.

74

mean that Jesus never assumed that part of our nature which is permanent, and this, as orthodox theology has always maintained, would mean that He did not truly become man. Fourthly, there is the point made so well by William Temple, 'To say that the Infant Jesus was from His cradle exercising providential care over it all (*i.e.* the universe) is certainly monstrous; but to deny this, and yet to say that the Creative Word was so self-emptied as to have no being except in the Infant Jesus, is to assert that for a certain period the history of the world was let loose from the control of the Creative Word, and "apart from Him" very nearly everything happened that happened at all during thirty odd years, both on this planet and throughout the immensities of space.'[1] Fifthly, the linguistic basis of the theory is not firm. It is not at all certain that 'he emptied himself' refers to the incarnation. It might well be a translation of 'he hath poured out his soul' in Isaiah 53:12, and be a reference to the death of the Lord.

The difficulties in the way of the theory seem insuperable. For our present inquiry the main point to notice is that it cannot be maintained that Paul was thinking of a Jesus who was no more than human. Philippians 2:5ff. is a passage which demands for its understanding that Jesus was divine in the fullest sense.

Cosmic functions

The passage we have just been considering involves the idea that Christ did not begin His existence when He was born in Bethlehem. He existed before ever He was born. Paul brings out this thought of His pre-existence on a number of occasions, as when he speaks of Jesus as being 'sent' into the world (Rom. 8:3; Gal. 4:4), or as 'becoming poor' for us (2 Cor. 8:9). In one remarkable passage he affirms that the Israelites of old in the wilderness 'drank from the supernatural Rock that followed them, and the Rock was Christ' (1 Cor. 10:4). It is true that this does not take us back into times eternal, but it does given an astonishing picture of Christ's tender care for the people of God centuries before His incarnation. Paul

[1] *Christus Veritas* (London, 1925), pp. 142f.

appears to be the first to make use of this idea of Christ's pre-existence, and Rawlinson thinks it so important that he speaks of it as the new element in Paul's thinking about Christ.[1]

In His pre-existent state Christ was associated with the work of creation. 'In him all things were created, in heaven and on earth, visible and invisible, whether thrones or dominions or principalities or authorities – all things were created through him and for him' (Col. 1:16; *cf.* 1 Cor. 8:6). This is a staggering assertion to be made about Him who walked the hills of Galilee. But Paul does not leave it there. He sustains this whole universe, for 'in him all things hold together' (Col. 1:17).

Perhaps we should add to this the thought that the doctrine of the Fall includes the idea of a fall of nature as well as of man. Consequently the Jews expected the Messiah to have as one of His functions the restoration of nature. 'The Messiah would have to be a figure of cosmic significance, capable of restoring the whole universe to its original condition, the master not only of man but of nature.'[2] Paul had no insignificant view of his Master. It was this gigantic cosmic function that he saw Him fulfilling (*cf.* Rom. 8:22f.). After all, if He had created it, and if He sustained it, should He not be able to restore it?

Christ's work for man

'The true key to Christ's person is in His work. . . . It lies in His personal action, and in our experience of saving benefits from Him . . . the forgiveness we take from Christ is taken directly from the hand and heart of God, immediately though not unmediated. Christ is God forgiving. He does not help us to God, He brings God. In Him God comes . . . God is Love only if Jesus is God. Otherwise Jesus would become our real God.' These words of P. T. Forsyth[3] remind us that Paul loved to dwell on the work of Christ. He felt that he himself owed everything to the Lord's saving work, and he found in this work the heart of the gospel that he preached. And this saving

[1] *Op. cit.*, p. 120.
[2] W. D. Davies, *op. cit.*, p. 39.
[3] *Positive Preaching and Modern Mind* (London, 1909), p. 353.

work is not the kind of activity that could be carried through by one who was simply man.

Persistently Paul links Christ's death with our sin. He 'died for our sins according to the scriptures' (1 Cor. 15: 3); He 'gave himself for our sins to deliver us from the present evil age' (Gal. 1: 4). Here we see the Lord's death as something planned from of old in the counsels of God, for it is spoken of in the ancient Scriptures. His atoning work is the subject of prophecy.

Then Paul assures us that the purpose of Christ's giving Himself for our sins is to deliver us. He is not thinking of deliverance on a small scale. It is the deliverance of all the people of God at all times and in all places from all their sins. Such a gigantic work demands a gigantic Person. Paul does not think of Him simply as great. Such a great One might be far removed from men, both in His nature and in His sympathies. In what is perhaps the most moving verse in Scripture Paul speaks of 'the Son of God, who loved me and gave himself for me' (Gal. 2: 20). The high and lofty One, whose death can affect such great things, yet stoops to know the individual. More, He loves him.

When Paul seeks to convey the significance of Christ's death for sin he racks his vocabulary to find words that will help. Sometimes he thinks of redemption (Rom. 3:24), drawing his imagery from the freeing of slaves. Again, he thinks of reconciliation (Col. 1: 20ff.), the process of making friends again after a quarrel. Or he recalls the sacrifices that had been offered on altars through the centuries, and speaks of Christ as a sacrifice (Eph. 5:2). What the sacrifices vainly hinted at, His death effectively accomplished. The process of propitiation (Rom. 3: 25, AV gives the correct translation) reminds us that the wrath of God is against every evil thing and every evil man. But Christ's death has averted that wrath from those who are 'in Christ'. Paul employs all the legal imagery behind justification (Rom. 5: 9), the process of legal acquittal. He points out the paradox that it is guilty, ungodly men who are acquitted (Rom. 4:5), for their acquittal depends on the fact that Christ has satisfied all the claims of the law for them. He goes back in thought to the time when Israel was delivered from Egypt. He remembers the sacrifice that was offered to avert the angel of death from the houses of the people of God, and he writes 'Christ, our paschal Lamb, has been sacrificed' (1 Cor. 5:7).

The catalogue might be multiplied. It is abundantly clear that Paul thought of Christ's work for men as many-sided. He has fully dealt with the problem of man's sin. He has brought believers out of the peril into which their sin had betrayed them. He has brought them into a place of security, and eternal security at that. Small wonder that Paul can speak of 'the unsearchable riches of Christ' (Eph. 3:8), and maintain that Christians have been blessed 'in Christ with every spiritual blessing in the heavenly places' (Eph. 1:3). Only a divine Saviour could accomplish all this.

Men's Attitude to Christ

Since they owe so much to Christ it is not surprising that believers are frequently exhorted to do things 'for Christ's sake'. For His sake they are slaves (such is the meaning of the word rendered 'servants' in 2 Cor. 4:5), which covers the whole of life. Every activity is thought of as in some way related to Christ, as an opportunity of doing Him service. Paul can go so far·as to say, 'to me to live is Christ' (Phil. 1:21). This relationship to Christ transforms the whole concept of suffering. It is a privilege to suffer for Him (Phil. 1:29). 'For the sake of Christ' Paul can take pleasure in such unlikely things as weaknesses, insults, hardships, persecutions, and calamities (2 Cor. 12:10).

Paul thought of Christ as the object of a specifically religious devotion. He himself freely prayed to Christ, and called on others to do the same (*e.g.* Rom. 10:12f.; 1 Cor. 1:2; 16:22; 2 Cor. 12:8; 1 Thes. 3:11f.; 2 Thes. 2:16f.; 3:5). This, in itself, marks out Christ as occupying the highest place. In similar vein is Paul's treatment of the sacraments, the two sacred rites of the Christians. Both baptism and the holy communion are closely associated with the Lord. Baptism is 'into Christ Jesus' (Rom. 6:3). The sacred meal which Christians kept is 'a participation in the blood of Christ ... a participation in the body of Christ' (1 Cor. 10:16). It can be called 'the Lord's supper' (1 Cor. 11:20).

And if the characteristic religious observances are closely

related to Christ, so is the church, the worshipping community. The church is Christ's church (Rom. 16:16). It is subject to Him (Eph. 5:24). But we are not to think of the church as an organization of men who are separate from and obedient to a supreme sovereign Lord. While Paul says nothing to diminish the sovereignty of Christ he yet insists on the thought that the church is in the closest of unions with its Lord. The church is His body, and He is the Head of the church (Eph. 1:22f.). Believers are 'united to the Lord' (1 Cor. 6:17).

From all this we see that the attitude that men should have to Christ is the attitude they should have to God.

Paul's 'Christ-mysticism'

Reference has often been made to what is called Paul's 'Christ-mysticism'. The term is not ideal, for Paul was no mystic in the usually accepted sense of the term. Nor is the way that he advocates properly called mysticism, for mysticism is necessarily the path of the few, whereas Paul speaks of experiences which he clearly expects all believers to share. But the expression turns our attention to Paul's firm conviction of the closeness of the union between Christ and believers.

The most important expression is 'in Christ' which occurs with great frequency. There has been much discussion of the exact force of the phrase. In an important work John Best maintains that it is closely linked with membership of the church.[1] Be that as it may, it certainly points us to the fact that the day by day life of the believer is lived in close contact with his Lord.

This truth is brought out in a variety of ways. Everyone knows that part of the Christian way of life is to abstain from all evil. But Paul puts it more forcibly than that. Paul remembers that his Master, to put away sin, died for His people. So he says that the Christian is crucified with Christ (Gal. 2: 20), that he has died with Christ (Col. 2: 20), that he is buried with Him in baptism (Rom. 6: 4; Col. 2: 12). Paul sees the Christian's act of renunciation as something done in the very closest connection with the Lord.

[1] One Body in Christ (London, 1955), chapter I.

But Christianity is not negative. It is not simply abstaining from the evil, but actively doing the good. If the believer has died to the old, he rises to the new. Paul expresses this by saying that he is made alive together with Christ (Eph. 2: 5), that he rises with Christ (Col. 3: 1). Now he lives with Christ (1 Thes. 5: 10), he has put on Christ (Rom. 13: 14). So sure is Paul that his own life is lived in immediate contact with the Lord that he tells us that Christ speaks in him (2 Cor. 13: 3) and that he speaks in Christ (2 Cor. 2: 17). He forgives 'in the presence of Christ' (2 Cor. 2: 10).

Behind all such statements is the conviction that Christ is divine, and as such, dwells and works in His people. There is no systematic working out of a theme, but there is the thought that wherever Christians are, and whatever they do, everything hinges on their relationship to the Lord. He has made them one with Himself. This is convincing evidence that Paul never regarded Christ as merely a man like himself, but recognized Him as his Lord and God.

The subordination of Christ to God

There are a few passages which are sometimes alleged to prove that Christ is not God in the fullest sense, for He occupies a place below that of the Father. Such are those which refer to 'the God of our Lord Jesus Christ' (Eph. 1: 17), or which expressly speak of Him as in some way subject to the Father. Thus in the climax to the process outlined in 1 Corinthians 15: 24ff. He is described as 'subjected to him who put all things under him, that God may be everything to every one'. Compare also 'the head of Christ is God' (1 Cor. 11: 3), and 'Christ is God's' (1 Cor. 3: 23). Sometimes we find the thought of the Father bestowing rewards upon Christ, *e.g.* 'Therefore God has highly exalted him' (Phil. 2: 9; *cf.* Rom. 15: 9; Col. 1: 19).

The first point we would lay down is that these few passages must be interpreted in the light of the great majority of the kind that we have been considering up till now. It is a 'methodological error' (to use the horrible modern jargon) to take a few expressions like these, which admit of more than one interpretation, and make of them a standard so that all others must be wrenched into conformity. Rather we must try to see Paul's thought as a whole. When we do, we see that essentially he places Christ with God. But at the same time he does not shrink from the proposition that in the Person of Christ God became man, man with all the limitations that that involves. He came to do a work in this world of space and time, and it is proper to think of Him as occupying a position of subordination while He was carrying out this task. As a man, He was subject to the Father. As a man, He could be rewarded and exalted. The exaltation is the seal set by the Father on the work of the Son. None of the passages we have cited sets out to give an account of the Son as He is in His essential nature. Each is concerned with Him as He appears in His work for man's redemption. Probably the most difficult of them is 1 Corinthians 15: 24ff. Yet when we look into it, this passage is plainly concerned with the work of Christ in time. He came to do a certain work, and that work will not be brought to its climax until all things and all people, including the Agent of that redemptive work, are subject to the Father. But Paul does not say that the Son in His essential nature is subject, and his words must not be held to imply this. When we bear in mind that he thought of Christ's manhood as real, and not as a piece of play-acting, we see that a certain subordination is not only explicable, but is positively demanded.

Conclusion

There can be no denying that Paul made a profound contribution to the Christian understanding of the Person of its Founder. We have not been able in this brief treatment to do more than indicate some of the more important aspects of his thought. Much, including much of importance, has necessarily been left unsaid. Paul penetrated deeply into the mystery of the Person of Christ, and all Christians everywhere are enriched by what the Spirit revealed to him.

Once again we see the two thoughts of the true manhood and the true Godhead held in balance. Paul does not simply repeat, parrot fashion, what others were saying. According to the gift given him, he was able to see more of what was involved in the incarnation. Yet the two essential points are the same. Jesus of Nazareth in the apostle's thought was genuinely a man. Paul made no attempt to gloss over the human experience of Jesus. The picture he gives us is not that of a demi-god walking the earth. But he combines with the thought of a true manhood the thought of the true deity of Jesus. 'God was in Christ' (2 Cor. 5: 19, AV, RSV margin). Paul speaks in the sight of God 'in Christ' (2 Cor. 12: 19). He refers to Christ as 'God blessed for ever' (Rom. 9: 5, AV). Again and again he holds out Christ before men as the object of faith (e.g. Gal. 2: 16; Eph. 1: 15; Phil. 3: 8f.). He associates Christ with the Father and the Spirit in passages which invite interpretations of a Trinitarian character (e.g. Rom. 8: 11; 15: 16; 1 Cor. 12: 4-6; 2 Cor. 13: 14; Eph. 2: 18; 4: 4-6; 2 Thes. 2: 13; Tit. 3: 4-6).[1]

In his own way, employing his own terminology, making use of his own profound insights into the deep things of God, he brings out of his treasure things new and old. But in the process he makes it clear that he is giving his own individual, emphatic expression to what is nothing other than the common Christian faith as to the Person of the Lord.

---

[1] A. E. J. Rawlinson says, 'If S. Paul's language is not always explicitly Trinitarian – and it would be absurd to expect to find in his writings a technical statement of the doctrine of the Trinity – his theology is nevertheless in a general sense Trinitarian in tendency' (op cit., p. 159).

6 A great High Priest

No part of the New Testament, with the possible exception of the apocalyptic passages, is more difficult for modern men to understand than the Letter to the Hebrews. Much of its imagery is borrowed from Jewish ritualism, with its priesthood, sacrifices and the like. Some of it is coloured by Greek philosophy. Thus we find ourselves simultaneously in two thought worlds which are not ours, and it is easy to feel that there is nobody to show us around. Not surprisingly, unless we are very determined, we soon get lost. So we tend to leave this Letter largely unread.

This is a great pity. For every part of the Bible has its contribution to make, and nothing can be neglected without loss. The message of the Letter to the Hebrews is very relevant to the needs of our day. Ours is an age of broad tolerance. Some generations have been so zealous for truth that they have delighted to define it narrowly, and then dub everybody 'heretic' who did not see it aright. Today we will have none of that! In every walk of life it is the broadminded, tolerant person who is admired (even if he is not always imitated!). In matters religious the common view is that all religions are right and all are wrong. All have some contribution to make to the truth, and none has all the truth. 'Comparative religion' has come to mean that field of study which sets comparable religious entities side by side. Christianity becomes no more than one of the world's great religions. But no Christian who has grasped the message of Hebrews could make that mistake.

It has usually been held that this Letter was written to a group of Jewish Christians who were in danger of slipping back into Judaism. They had been Christians for some time, and might well have been leaders in the faith. But instead, their minds were being directed to the attractiveness of the religion of their fathers, and they were contemplating a return to it. In modern times some great scholars have abandoned this interpretation. But, as A. M. Stibbs remarks, attempts to show that the Letter was written in the first place to Gentiles are 'more ingenious than convincing'.[1] The writer of the Letter sets out to demolish the idea that there is as much to be said for Judaism as for Christianity. His great theme is that Christianity is and must of necessity be the final religion. For God is in it in a special way. There is all the difference in the world between a religion which rests on what God has revealed through great men of old, and that which is the result of the revelation and the atonement wrought by His Son. The writer starts from the Person of Christ and goes on to point out the finality of the religion which results from what He did. But as our concern is with what he thought about the Lord, we have to reverse the process. His beliefs about Christ's Person must be deduced from his account of Christ's work.

Again and again our author refers to Christ in terms of priesthood. He is 'a merciful and faithful high priest in the service of God' (2:17). He is 'a great high priest who has passed through the heavens' (4:14). He is 'a high priest, one who is seated at the right hand of the throne of the Majesty in heaven' (8:1). There is much more. Nor would we have the complete picture if we were simply to take a concordance and look up all the passages where 'priest' or 'high priest' occurs. The idea is present even where the actual words do not occur. So completely does the idea of the high-priestly work of Christ dominate the Letter that Alexander Nairne could entitle his study of it, *The Epistle of Priesthood*. Now not everyone would make a high priest. Important qualifications are necessary. It is one of the points of this Letter that our Lord had all the qualifications.

[1] *New Bible Commentary* (London, 1953), p. 1088.

The humanity of Jesus

It is required in every high priest 'chosen from among men' that he 'can deal gently with the ignorant and wayward, since he himself is beset with weakness' (5: 1f.). This leads to a strong emphasis on our Lord's genuine humanity. Indeed, there is probably no book in the New Testament that emphasizes the humanity more strongly than does this Letter.

The writer delights to use the human name 'Jesus', and almost invariably he puts it in an emphatic position. By itself (*i.e.* without such an addition as 'Christ') this name points us to the Man, Jesus. The emphatic position focuses attention on the reality and the importance of His true humanity. We are never allowed to forget that Jesus 'for a little while was made lower than the angels' (2: 9). The purpose of this was 'the suffering of death'. References to His death are numerous, and they all remind us that Jesus was true Man, for God does not die.

More than once the significance of His temptations is brought out. In 2: 18 the reality of His sufferings and temptations means that 'he is able to help those who are tempted'. He has a genuine sympathy with us, and a personal knowledge of what it is like to suffer temptation. His temptation was not of an unusual kind, for 'in every respect (he) has been tempted as we are, yet without sin' (4: 15). It is a scriptural principle that 'God cannot be tempted with evil' (Jas. 1: 13). These temptations accordingly point us to a real Man.

But the most striking passage is 5: 7ff. Here we read of 'the days of his flesh', His 'prayers and supplications', His 'loud cries and tears', His fear, His learning of obedience through what He suffered, and His being made perfect. Not very many people feel quite at home using language of this kind about the Lord. The fact that our writer employs it so easily and naturally shows how clearly he perceived the genuineness of Christ's humanity. Only one who was perfectly sure of it would speak in this way. His idea of Christ's being made perfect must not be misconstrued. Neither here nor in 2: 10, where he says that our Lord was made perfect 'through suffering', does he mean that Christ was once imperfect, and that He was brought out of that state. There is the perfection of the bud, which is not the same as the perfection of the flower into which in course of time it grows. The word 'made perfect' has about it the idea of reaching one's proper end or aim (sometimes it refers to becoming mature). Our writer means that Jesus was brought to His consummation through sufferings. The perfect Boy became the perfect Man. And the perfect Man became the perfect Saviour only through the path of suffering.

All this is important as constituting one of Jesus' qualifications to be our High Priest. A high priest must know the limitations of those he represents. He must be touched with their infirmities. In Jesus 'we have not a high priest who is unable to sympathize with our weaknesses' (4:15). He was Himself man, and He knows the weakness of our frame. Our author explicitly relates this to His priesthood: 'he had to be made like his brethren in every respect, so that he might become a merciful and faithful high priest in the service of God' (2:17). The humanity of Jesus is not something to be explained away or glossed over. The writer 'thinks of the sojourn on earth as not merely a temporary eclipse and humiliation, but as the indispensable prelude to the heavenly life'.[1] Genuine humanity is an integral part of the pattern of priesthood.

The divine appointment

The honour of being high priest is not open to man's ambition. No man can take it upon himself (5:4). The high priest ministers in such holy matters that only God can appoint him. Thus it was that Aaron, for example, was called of God to this task. He did not take it upon himself; nor did Moses make him high priest. God called him to this work, and no one else could have done so. In the same way, 'Christ did not exalt himself to be made a high priest' (5:5). He was a High Priest because God made Him so. He was 'called of God' (5:10) to this office.

But if Christ was like earthly high priests in owing His position to the divine appointment, He surpassed them in that it was confirmed with a divine oath (7:20). His priesthood is permanent. There was no equivalent oath in the case of the Aaronic priesthood, and in due course that priesthood gave way

[1] E. F. Scott, *The Epistle to the Hebrews* (Edinburgh, 1923), p. 148.

to another, namely, that of our Lord. The oath means that Christ's priesthood will not pass away. It superseded the Aaronic priesthood, but nothing will ever supersede it. God has sworn and His oath must stand.

The order of Melchizedek

We have looked at some of our Lord's qualifications for priesthood. We turn our attention now to the nature of His priesthood. Perplexing to modern men is the repeated statement that Christ was a High Priest 'after the order of Melchizedek'. They do not see what it means, and they do not see what it matters. But we must grapple with it if we would understand the thought of this Letter.

Melchizedek is a mysterious figure. We hear of him only in Genesis 14: 18-20. He flashes across the scene like a meteor. There is no heralding of his appearance, nor any mention of its results. There is no account of his family. There is no account of his work. We learn only that he was king of Salem and priest of God Most High. When Abraham was returning from his victory over the kings, Melchizedek met him with bread and wine. The priest blessed the patriarch, and received from him a tithe of the spoils of war. Then he vanished from the scene as suddenly as he had appeared.

He was not forgotten, for we read concerning the Messiah in Psalm 110: 4, that 'the Lord hath sworn and will not change his mind, "You are a priest for ever after the order of Melchizedek" '. But this is a solitary instance. Evidently the thinkers and the writers of the ancient world found him too mysterious a figure to make anything of him. Not so the writer of this Letter.

He is particularly interested in the point, unusual among Semitic peoples, and very unusual among Semitic priests, that there is neither genealogy nor posterity recorded of this man. This leads to the thought that He who is Priest after the order of Melchizedek has neither beginning nor successor. 'No beginning' raises in our mind thoughts of pre-existence and deity. 'No successor' is another way of indicating that here we have the final religion. This Priest will never be superseded as was Aaron.

87

It is repeatedly said that His priesthood after the order of Melchizedek is 'for ever' (5:6; 6:20; 7:17, 21). Once we are reminded of the oath, 'The Lord has sworn and will not change his mind' (7:21). 'He holds his priesthood permanently' (7:24); it is 'inviolable', as the RV margin says. Westcott comments, 'Christ's Priesthood is His alone, open to no rival claim, liable to no invasion of its functions.'[1]

Sometimes there is a stress on the quality of our Lord's life. He 'continues a priest for ever' (7: 3; it is Melchizedek who is made like Him, not He like Melchizedek). He 'continues for ever', and 'always lives' (7: 24f.). His priesthood is 'not according to a legal requirement concerning bodily descent but by the power of an indestructible life' (7:16). The Aaronic priests function only on the basis of outward conformity to the Law's requirements ('according to a legal requirement concerning bodily descent'). By contrast Christ's priesthood is *akatalutos*, 'indestructible'. 'Endless', the AV rendering of this word, is not adequate. It means not only 'which does not end', but 'which cannot end'. It refers to the quality of His life as indissoluble. This quality of life is the basis of His priesthood.

The greatness of this priesthood is obvious. Its superiority to all Levitical priesthood is underlined with a reference to the tithes Abraham paid to Melchizedek (7: 4ff.), and to the blessing given to the patriarch. The Levitical priests received tithes from the people. But, so to speak, Levi, from whom they were all descended, paid tithes to Melchizedek while he was in the loins of his progenitor Abraham. In this way the Levitical priesthood symbolically paid tribute to the priesthood of Melchizedek, and recognized its superiority. The same point is made with respect to the blessing. 'It is beyond dispute that the inferior is blessed by the superior' (7:7), which makes Melchizedek 'superior' to Abraham, though Abraham was the forefather of the people of God.

In such ways the immeasurable greatness of the Priest 'after the order of Melchizedek' is brought out. The two great thoughts are those of the permanence of this priesthood, and the greatness of the Priest. The greatness is so very great that it

[1] *Commentary, in loc.*

lifts Him out of the sphere of the merely human. It is not too much to say, with Vincent Taylor, that 'High Priest' as used in Hebrews, 'describes One who is worshipped and adored, and, in consequence, is divine as well as human'.[1]

The shadow and the substance

At this point it may be well to notice the use our author makes of some current philosophical concepts. The extent of his knowledge of Greek philosophy is disputed, and there is no reason for thinking that he was a deeply learned philosopher. But some philosophical concepts had come to be familiar terms in educated society (as in the case of some scientific terms today) Our writer makes some use of one or two of them.

Plato had spoken of the perfect heavenly 'ideas' of which things on earth are but the imperfect copies and counterparts. Plato's thought is far too complex to do justice to it in a paragraph. But we may, perhaps, illustrate the impression it left on more ordinary men. The easiest thing is to start with some common object, say, a table. The 'idea' of the table, the really perfect table, is in heaven. All earthly tables are at best imperfect copies or shadows of the heavenly reality. They vaguely reveal to us something of what 'table' means. They point us to the perfect 'idea', that heavenly table which alone is 'table' in the fullest sense. They are not the real table, though, as shadows, they point us to the substance, the genuine heavenly article. This is true of all earthly objects, for everything has its heavenly counterpart. The earthly copy is always shadowy and imperfect. The heavenly reality alone is perfect.

This kind of thinking influenced a number of Jewish scholars, especially Philo and the Alexandrians generally. While the writer to the Hebrews was undoubtedly influenced much more by Old Testament ideas than by current philosophy, yet he finds this idea a useful one. There are references in the Old Testament to the pattern of the tabernacle shown to Moses (Ex. 25:9, 40; Nu. 8:4). In the Old Testament the point is made that the tabernacle is rather wonderful, because it is a copy of the heavenly. But for our writer the point is that it is

1 *The Names of Jesus* (London, 1953), p. 115.

only a copy. He quotes this very command to Moses to make everything according to the pattern shown him, to demonstrate that the Levitical priests serve only the 'copy and shadow of the heavenly sanctuary' (8:5). Jesus, by contrast, was 'a minister in the sanctuary and the true tent which is set up not by man but by the Lord' (8:2). The holy place which is 'made with hands' is nothing but 'a copy of the true one', whereas Christ entered 'into heaven itself, now to appear in the presence of God on our behalf' (9:24; cf. 9:11). This explicit contrast between the earthly and the heavenly sanctuaries stresses the difference between the ministers in the two. Because Christ's priesthood is that of the perfect heavenly sanctuary it is obvious that Christ's Person cannot be comprehended in merely human categories.

The same contrast that we see between the earthly and the heavenly sanctuaries and the earthly and the heavenly priesthoods is drawn also between the earthly and the heavenly offerings. The tabernacle of old was only 'symbolic'. The offerings made in it were 'gifts and sacrifices . . . which cannot perfect the conscience of the worshipper' (9:9). At best such offerings could purify 'the copies of the heavenly things' (9:23). They could point to the heavenly reality, but they were not, themselves, that reality. Thus it is that in them is made 'a reminder of sin' (10:3). But our author asserts flatly that 'it is impossible that the blood of bulls and goats should take away sins' (10:4). Thus, when dealing with the sacrifices offered by the Levitical priesthood, the writer to the Hebrews follows a clear and consistent line. These offerings do not and cannot take away sin. They are no more than shadows. But the shadow points to the substance, and so these offerings point us to the one perfect sacrifice that really does take away sins.

And that perfect sacrifice is the one offered by Christ. More than once we are reminded that Christ did not offer some other victim (as the Levitical priests, of course, did), but He offered Himself (9:12, 26). The animal victims were really very inferior offerings. Over against their total inability to atone for sins our author sets the fact that Christ came to do the will of God (10:3–9). This is often interpreted as meaning that the essence of Christ's sacrifice is that it was the sacrifice of obedience. We would not wish to minimize the importance of this aspect of His offering, but our author goes on to point out that the will of God which He obeyed was that prescribing 'the offering of the body of Jesus Christ' (10:10). It was necessary not only that Christ should live obediently and die obediently, but that He should offer His body. Thus was consummated the perfect sacrifice, offered by the perfect Priest.

Christ's work for men

The effect of Christ's offering was to obtain for men 'eternal redemption' (9:12). That is to say, His offering has brought to man a redemption that cannot be improved upon. It is perpetual in its efficacy. Our author delights to bring out the decisive character of our Lord's offering. We saw earlier that he thought of Christ's priesthood as the ultimate and permanent priesthood. The same could be said about His offering. It was final and decisive. The word *hapax* is used to convey the thought that the offering was 'once for all' (9:26, 28). The strengthened form, *ephapax*, which says the same thing, but says it more emphatically, is applied to His sacrifice in 7:27; 9:12; and 10:10. Where Christ has offered 'there is no longer any offering for sin' (10:18).

The Letter opens with a reminder that the Son 'made purification for sins' (1:3). As the Letter unfolds, this thought is reiterated in a variety of ways. His work was 'to make expiation (RV, 'propitiation') for the sins of the people' (2:17). More than once the great prophecy of the new covenant is cited from Jeremiah 31. It is quoted at length in 8:8ff., and in an abbreviated form in 10:16f. The interesting point is that both times our author stops with the words which deal with the forgiveness of sins. That was what Christ had come to effect. That was what He did effect. His great work for men was to put away their sin completely. They may now have 'confidence to enter into the sanctuary by the blood of Jesus' (10:19). No wonder that he can refer shortly to what Christ has wrought as 'such a great salvation' (2:3).

Conclusion

We are in no danger of treating Hebrews as a re-hash of the teaching we see elsewhere in the New Testament. This Letter moves in a thought world of its own. Its categories of priesthood, of earthly shadows pointing to heavenly perfections, of types and figures, are unique. Yet when we take the trouble to distinguish between form and content, and to penetrate to the meaning of the imagery used, we see that the author's essential view of Christ is that of the other writers we have studied. He is sure of the genuine manhood of Jesus, none surer. But equally he ascribes to Him such functions and accords Him such a place as none but God Himself can perform and occupy.

7   God the Word

1. The Gospel according to John

St John's Gospel makes easy reading, especially in a modern
translation. But its simplicity is deceptive. These words which
even a child can understand express thoughts so profound that
the wisest among us will scarcely claim to have plumbed them
to the depths. Take for example John 14:2, 'In my Father's
house are many rooms.' This passage may be read in the lowly
cottages of ignorant and unlearned folk, in the sure knowledge
that it will be understood. And yet, what do these words really
mean? A complete answer seems impossible. Again and again
John presents us with this paradox. His Gospel is at once the
simplest and most difficult of the four. Here, even more than in
other parts of the Bible, we must content ourselves with noting
some of the more obvious features of his testimony and refrain
from any attempt to fathom completely the depths of his
thought.

The Logos
The Gospel opens with the baffling statement, 'In the beginning
was the Word.' This imagery is foreign to us. We hardly know
what to make of it. But the term 'Logos' (Word) was common
in the first century, and J. H. Bernard can say, 'We may be sure
that the Logos of God was as familiar a topic in the educated
circles of Asia Minor as the doctrine of Evolution is in Europe
or America at the present day, and was discussed not only by
the learned but by half-instructed votaries of many religions.'[1]

1 *The Gospel According to St John (ICC)* (Edinburgh, 1928), p. cxlii.

The philosophers, who were more or less the ancient equivalent of our scientists, used 'Logos' in a variety of ways. Heraclitus spoke of 'the omnipresent Wisdom by which all things are steered', which almost implies conscious will, and so means something very like God. More usually the idea of personality was excluded. The Stoics often referred to the *spermatikos logos*, which means something like 'generative wisdom'. This signified a kind of divine reason, operative within nature and man. Ordinary people would not understand all this, but they would understand that the philosophers thought highly of the Logos.

The Jews independently used the same 'word' concept in a most interesting way. At this time many of them no longer spoke Hebrew, the language of their sacred Scripture, but Aramaic. However, in their synagogues, the Scripture was always read in its original Hebrew. In order that the people might understand it, running translations (called 'Targums') were made into Aramaic. Now the Jews paid great respect to the commandment not to take the Lord's name in vain. In a laudable endeavour to ensure that they never did this they completely gave up using the divine name. They substituted some reverent periphrasis like 'the Lord', 'the Blessed', 'the Holy One'. One of these periphrases was 'the Word', and this was used in some of the Targums. Thus we read that our first parents heard 'the voice of the Word of God' walking in the garden (Gn. 3:8), and that Jacob took 'the Word of the Lord' to be his God (Gn. 28:21). So, where the Targums were in use, people were accustomed to hearing 'the Word of the Lord' as equivalent to God Himself.

The process would have been helped by the fact that in the Old Testament the 'word' is spoken of as doing things. For example, the word of the Lord comes to people (Gn. 15:1; Ezk. 3:16, *etc.*). The word of the Lord was responsible for creation (Ps. 33:6).[1]

[1] The Rabbis ascribed a very large function to 'the Word', 'the Law' (which was much the same, Isaiah 2: 3) and 'the Wisdom', treating them much like extensions of the Divine. See Sir E. Hoskyns, *The Fourth Gospel* (London, 1950), p. 155, for some of the evidence.

The importance of the 'Logos' or 'Word' in the terminology of the time may be gauged from its frequent use in the writings of Philo, the learned Jew of Alexandria, a man who embodied the cultures both of Judaism and Hellenism. According to W. F. Howard he uses 'Logos' thirteen hundred times,[1] and in a variety of ways. One way of especial importance to us is to denote 'God Himself as revealed'.[2] God's essential being is unknowable. But God's Logos is His thought issuing in activities of many kinds, and revealing Him to men.

The prologue to St John's Gospel must be understood against such a background. John could write knowing that, whether his readers were Greeks or Jews, they would appreciate his reference to the Logos. They would understand that he was claiming that Jesus of Nazareth was responsible for all creation (1:3), and for giving men the true light (1:4, 9). John took over the divine associations of the term, and added to them the notion of personality. For him the Logos was no less than God (1:1).

The Father and the Son

John habitually refers to Jesus as 'the Son', and this term is also significant. He thinks of Jesus as standing in a specially close relationship to the Father (*cf.* the fourfold reference to Jesus as the 'only Son', 1:14, 18; 3:16, 18). Jesus said, 'I and the Father are one' (10:30), and again, 'he who sees me sees him who sent me' (12:45). Philip, who does not seem to have been the brightest of men, made a request in the upper room, 'Lord, show us the Father, and we shall be satisfied' (14:8), only to receive the answer, 'he who has seen me has seen the Father' (14:9).

John paints for us a picture in which the Son and the Father are in the closest possible connection. Jesus perfectly reveals the Father. That lies behind His words to Philip. There is unity of will and purpose, so that Jesus always does the Father's will

---

[1] *Christianity According to St John* (London, 1943), pp. 36f.
[2] C. H. Dodd, *The Interpretation of the Fourth Gospel* (Cambridge, 1953), p. 277. A. W. Argyle is of the opinion that Philo thought of the Logos as personal. *Expository Times*, LXVI, pp. 13f.

(5:30; 8:28). The Christ of whom John writes is absolutely one with His Father.

This is not affected by the fact that Jesus occupies a lowly place as He walks among men. John is not unmindful of the fact that the Son had enjoyed the glory of the Father 'before the world was made' (17:5), and that He had left all this. But one of the great thoughts of the Fourth Gospel is that in Jesus' very lowliness and humility the true glory is to be seen. Those who had eyes to see beheld it (1:14). They saw it in the mighty works, the 'signs' (2:11; 11:40). They saw it in Jesus' whole manner of life. At the end He could say that His path of lowly service had shown forth the glory of God (17:4).

John does not hesitate to take this thought right through to its logical conclusion. Crucifixion was synonymous with shame and degradation and humiliation. But John tells us that when the cross was in immediate prospect Jesus said, 'The hour has come for the Son of man to be glorified' (12:23), and again, 'Now is the Son of man glorified, and in him God is glorified; if God is glorified in him, God shall also glorify him in himself, and glorify him at once' (13:31f.). This is not easy to grasp on a first reading because of the repetition of the same words 'glorify' and 'glorified'. But the main points are clear. The cross meant the glorifying of the Son, and it meant also the glorifying of the Father. In the words of William Temple, 'If God is love, His glory most of all shines forth in whatever most fully expresses love. The Cross of shame *is* the throne of glory.'[1]

The claims of Christ

Note the seven occurrences of the phrase 'I am': 'I am the bread of life' (6:35), 'I am the light of the world' (8:12), 'I am the door' (10:7, 9), 'I am the good shepherd' (10:11), 'I am the resurrection and the life' (11:25), 'I am the way, and the truth, and the life' (14:6), 'I am the true vine' (15:1). In each case the Greek form of 'I am' is emphatic. There is no need to include the personal pronoun in such an expression in Greek unless emphasis is required. But it is found in each of these sayings. To Jewish ears this 'I am' aroused associations of the divine, for

[1] *Readings in St John's Gospel* (London, 1947), p. 14.

in the Greek translation of the Hebrew Old Testament, the expression is frequently used by God Himself. There is little doubt that John's repeated use of this expression is meant to awaken these divine associations.

The content of the sayings matches the form. We have not the space here to engage in a systematic exegesis, but even a casual reading shows that they express a large claim. They assert the Son's ability to supply man's deep needs. We may perhaps appreciate something of their far-reaching implications if we try to imagine anyone else making use of such words. The very idea is preposterous. The words imply a consciousness of powers more than human. And, extraordinary as they are, they do not stand alone. Jesus also said, 'If anyone keeps my word, he will never see death' (8:51). He claimed that He could give men life, and that 'abundantly' (10:10). And more beside.

Jesus claimed extraordinary knowledge. Sometimes this had to do simply with facts, as when he knew that the woman of Samaria had had five husbands (4:18), that Lazarus was dead (11:14), or that Peter would deny Him (13:38). Before the feeding of the multitude He knew what He would do (6:6), and before the arrest He knew 'all that was to befall him' (18:4). Sometimes this knowledge was of a different kind. Several times He said He knew the Father in a way that others did not (7:29; 8:55; 17:25). His words in 10:15, 'as the Father knows me . . . I know the Father', indicate the very closest communion, as well as perfect knowledge. In connection with His mission He knew many things. He knew that the testimony borne to Him was true (5:32), He 'knew from the first who those were that did not believe, and who it was that would betray him' (6:64; cf. 13:11). He knew His sheep (10:14, 27). He knew that the Father 'had given all things into his hands' (13:3). Small wonder that at the end the disciples should say, 'Now we know that you know all things' (16:30).

In all this we see Jesus serenely conscious of His high dignity. As He walked among men He knew that there was that about His essential being which put Him above those around Him, and indeed, above all men. Without flamboyance, easily and naturally, He made the most astounding claims. He possessed such a deep insight into the deep things of God that these claims sound natural. They leave no doubt as to His close kinship to the Father.

Christ's work for men

Sometimes John's approach to our Lord's work is contrasted with that of Paul. It is said that Paul thinks of Jesus as redeeming men, while John regards Him primarily as revealing the Father. There is a certain plausibility about this, but it is wrong to overlook John's deep interest in the Lord's atoning work. As early as his first chapter he records the words (spoken by the Baptist), 'Behold, the Lamb of God, who takes away the sin of the world' (1:29). Probably the best-known text in the whole Bible is John. 3:16, the gospel 'in a nutshell'. And this interest, proclaimed thus early, is maintained throughout the Gospel. It is no accident that John mentions 'sin' more often than any of the other evangelists, more often, indeed, than Matthew and Mark put together. Sin matters to John. It is a serious problem. And it was the mission of Jesus to overcome that problem. So it is that John records the triumphant cry of Jesus at the moment of His death, 'It is finished' (19: 30). The work of atonement was done. Christ had completed the work He came to do.

This interest in the death of the Lord comes out in other ways. In chapter 10 we read of Jesus as the Good Shepherd. This is an aspect of our Lord's ministry which makes a wide appeal. Many have been the artists who have depicted Christ leading His sheep, or carrying a lamb. It is a vivid imagery, and brings before us many thoughts like the tender care Christ has for His own, the provision He makes for their needs to be met, and so on. But in John 10 the point which is emphasized is that 'the good shepherd lays down his life for the sheep' (verses 11, 15, 17, 18). This would take place only on the rarest occasions among human shepherds, but Jesus gives it as the characteristic thing about Himself as the Good Shepherd.

Even the words of the Lord's enemies are used to fasten attention on the same point. John records the words of Caiaphas, 'it is expedient for you that one man should die for the people, and that the whole nation should not perish' (11:50).

As Caiaphas meant them the words are sheer political expediency. They are the utterance of a cynic. 'Better that one man should die, even if He be innocent of any wrongdoing, than that the whole nation be brought into serious trouble with the Romans.' But John understands the words in a different sense. He sees in them a prophecy which God made His high priest to utter. The death of Jesus is vicarious. It is the means whereby He was 'to gather into one the children of God who are scattered abroad' (11:52). It is a mighty work of redemption.

The reason for the death of the Lord was that whoever believes in Him should not perish but have eternal life (3:16). Eternal life is one of John's great themes. It is mentioned with great frequency, and obviously mattered a great deal to the author. He associates it habitually with the Son. Again and again we are told that the way to eternal life is through believing in Him. John speaks once or twice of believing in the Father (5:24; 14:1), but this serves only to underline the closeness of the connection between the Father and the Son. Eternal life is the gift of the Son. It is a present possession, for the Son bestows it now on those who put their trust in Him.

The gifts He gives to His own are many and varied. He gives them the right to become 'the sons of God' (1:12; 'power' here is *exousia*, 'authority' or 'right'). Believers receive 'from his fulness' (1:16). They receive grace and truth (1:16f.). Christ gives living water (4:10). He is the bread of life (6:35). Those who come to Him will neither hunger nor thirst again (*ibid.*). He cast no-one out (6:37). None will snatch His people from His hand (10:28), nor from His Father's hand (10:29). When He left this world it was to prepare a place for them (14:2). Peace (14:27) and joy (15:11) are His gifts. Fruitful lives are lived by those who abide in Him (15:5).

Christ the Source of life
One of the features of the Fourth Gospel is the way John takes simple words, words like 'light' and 'life', words that everyone can understand, and makes them ring through his Gospel until you wonder why you ever thought them simple. Take, for example, life. In his opening words he tells us that 'in him was

life, and the life was the light of men' (1: 4). Twice we read that Jesus is 'the life' (11: 25; 14: 6). Again, 'as the Father has life in himself, so has he granted the Son also to have life in himself' (5: 26). Since He is thus the source of life, He comes to give men abundant life (10: 10). Frequently we read that eternal life comes from Him. Once it is defined as consisting in the knowledge of the Father and the Son (17: 3). The gift of life is associated with both the living water that He gives (4: 14) and with the bread of life, which is also His gift (6: 33, 51). Life is associated with eating His flesh and drinking His blood (6: 54). On one memorable occasion when many stumbled and ceased to follow Jesus, Peter refused to go away, saying, 'Lord, to whom shall we go? You have the words of eternal life' (6: 68). Clearly life, for John, is a many splendoured thing. And just as clearly its many splendours come from Christ. Outside Him there is no life at all.

Much more could be said. But this is sufficient to show that a great number of gifts, and gifts of a far-reaching nature, come from the Son. In His life and in His death He made available for men all kinds of blessings, culminating in that eternal life which alone is real life.

The sovereign Lord

John does not minimize the poverty and obscurity and lowliness in which the Master lived, nor the fact that His enemies resisted Him until they finally succeeded in getting Him put on a cross. Yet he manages to convey the other thought that Jesus is completely the Master of every situation. Take, for example, that matter of His being hounded to His death. In a sense that displayed the vindictiveness of His foes. But Jesus was quite clear that He would die as and when He pleased (10: 18). He said He would lay down His life and take it again. Then He proceeded to do just that. When He was ready, He told Judas to get on with the work of betrayal (13: 27).

This characteristic is to be discerned throughout the Gospel. Jesus assumes the right to change Simon's name (1: 42), and to call Philip (1: 43). He commands the servants to fill the waterpots (2: 7), and both on this and on other occasions works His miracles with sovereign hand. He takes it upon Himself to drive the traders out of the Temple (2:14ff.). He tells Nicodemus that he *must* be born again if he would see the kingdom of God (3:3, 7). He speaks with Pilate about His Kingdom (18:36f.), and there are several references to Him as King, which, while not meant seriously by the speakers, have been recorded for their deeper meaning (19:3, 14, 15, 19).

There is a very interesting series of passages referring to Jesus' 'hour' or His 'time'.[1] In the earlier part of the Gospel these tell us that His hour had not yet come. But when the cross is in immediate prospect Jesus says, 'the hour has come'. Men might rage how they pleased. His purpose was not affected. Nothing could interrupt His unhurried movement to His destined end.

Conclusion

Throughout this Gospel there are abundant evidences of John's belief in the kinship of Jesus with the Father. 'For John, Jesus' sonship does indeed involve a metaphysical relationship with the Father. . . . Undoubtedly he believes that the Son of God who was incarnate in Jesus of Nazareth inhabited eternity with the Father.'[2] The evidence comes in a variety of shapes, and is all the more impressive for that.

But John does not minimize the genuine manhood of Jesus. Just as truly as the other evangelists he pictures a Man among men. He has his own way of stressing the manhood, as when he speaks of Jesus not simply as the Word taking a body, or becoming man, but becoming 'flesh' (1:14, *cf.* the references to His flesh in chapter 6). Again and again He is spoken of as a 'man' (1:30; 4:29; 5:12; 8:40, *etc.*).

A noteworthy feature of the Johannine portrait is Jesus' habitual dependence on the Father. 'The son can do nothing of his own accord' (5: 19), 'I can do nothing on my own authority' (5:30). So marked is this that Hodgson can speak of this

---

[1] 2:4; 7:6, 8, 30; 8:20; 12:23, 27; 13:1; 17:1.
[2] C. K. Barrett, *The Gospel according to St. John* (London, 1955), p.60.

dependence as the 'keynote of our Lord's thought'.[1]

John records Jesus' weariness at Sychar (4:6), His emotion at the tomb of Lazarus (11:33, 35; W. F. Howard speaks of 'the shuddering horror and the tears at the tomb of Lazarus'[2]). So marked is John's emphasis on the very real humanity of Jesus that it is usually held that one of his aims in writing the Gospel was to combat docetism, the heresy that Jesus was not really a man, but only seemed to be one.

It is this thought of the real manhood that probably explains the references to the Son's being 'sent', and to His receiving gifts from the Father's hand. At any rate, it is clear enough that John thinks of a Christ who is really one with man and who is really one with God. He does not attempt to explain or reconcile these two points of view (unless we take 'the Word became flesh' as an explanation). But he gives clear expression to both, and we cannot ignore either if we are to be true to his thought.

2. The Letters of John

In the ancient world there were people who were firmly convinced that matter is evil. Only spirit is good, they thought, and since God is spirit and good He cannot possibly have any contact with this world of evil matter and with men who have evil, material bodies. If Jesus had a real body He could not be God. If He was God He could not be man. The one automatically rules the other out.

It is plain that in the circles where John moved there were some who held ideas like these. But John will have none of it. He insists that Jesus was both God and man. He goes as far as to say that it is the test of a man or of a spirit whether this truth is accepted. Any spirit from God 'confesses that Jesus Christ has come in the flesh', whereas a spirit of antichrist does not (1 Jn. 4:2f.; see also 2:22; 4:15; 5:1).

Right at the beginning of his first Letter John uncompromisingly takes up this position. He refers to Jesus as 'the word of life', and, as we saw in the section on the Gospel, 'the Word' is a

[1] *And Was Made Man* (London, 1938), p. 198.
[2] *Op. cit.*, p. 66.

title that indicates divinity. John underlines this point with his further statement that 'the life was made manifest' and his reference to 'the eternal life which was with the Father'. But we should also notice that in these same verses he speaks of this glorious Being as 'heard', 'seen', 'looked upon', 'touched with our hands' and 'made manifest'. Plainly he will have nothing to do with his opponents' demand: 'Either God or man'. He cheerfully responds, 'Both God and man'.

The atonement

We see something of the greatness of John's Lord from the work he sees Him as accomplishing for men. Jesus cleanses men from sin (1 Jn. 1: 7). Sins are forgiven 'for his sake' (1 Jn. 2: 12). He 'appeared to take away sins' (1 Jn. 3: 5). 'The reason the Son of God appeared was to destroy the works of the devil' (1 Jn. 3: 8), where both the title used and the work done are eloquent of John's high regard for the Christ. Again, he tells us that Jesus is our 'advocate with the Father' (1 Jn. 2: 1). 'Advocate' is a legal term, with a meaning like our 'counsel for the defence'. Its use brings out the thought that our hope is in Him and His work on our behalf.

Twice John calls Jesus 'the propitiation for our sins' (1 Jn. 2:2; 4:10; RSV translates otherwise, but this is the meaning of the Greek; it is concerned with putting away wrath). The term directs attention to the seriousness of sin. The wrath of God, the settled hostility of God's holy nature, is necessarily exercised towards everything evil. God is not simply mildly displeased about sin. He is angry about it and vigorously opposed to it. But Jesus is the means of dealing with sin and thus turning the divine wrath from us. He has provided the way to fellowship with God. This proceeds directly from the divine love, for the second of our two passages tells us that we know love only because God acted in this way in Christ to put away our sins. All of this is summed up in the wonderful title given Jesus, 'the Saviour of the world' (1 Jn. 4: 14).

The Father and the Son

Quite in the manner of the Gospel these Letters link the Father and the Son. Qualities like grace, mercy and peace come from them both (2 Jn. 3). He who abides in Christ's doctrine 'has' both the Father and the Son (2 Jn. 9). The Epistles have much to say about 'abiding', and it does not seem to make much difference whether the thought is completed with 'in the Father' or 'in the Son'. To take the opposite course and deny the Son is to cut oneself off from the Father (1 Jn. 2:23).

Clearly the Christology of the Letters does not differ from that of the Gospel. Both stress such functions of the Christ and such close relationship to the Father that we must think of Him as God. Both lay emphasis also on His genuine humanity. Both picture Christ as God become man for man's salvation.

3. The Revelation to John

Vivid imagery marks this book. There are powerful representations of scenes both in heaven and on earth. And dominating them is One whose characteristic designation is 'the Lamb'. We should not be misled by the associations of meekness which this term conjures up for us. In the apocalypses generally a lamb is the symbol of a conqueror. The Lamb in Revelation is an exalted Being. Though His death is not overlooked ('a Lamb . . . as though it had been slain', 5:6), this does not detract from His triumph in any way. It is precisely through His death that the triumph comes (7:14ff.; 12:11).

The names of Jesus
Our Lord is hailed in this book with a number of distinctive titles. He is 'Alpha and Omega' (1:11; 22:13), a title which is also used of God (1:8; 21:6). These are the first and last letters of the Greek alphabet. Thus this name is a pictorial way of saying that He is 'the beginning and the end', or 'the first and the last', expressions which also occur, as a matter of fact (e.g. 2:8). All this points us to His pre-eminence, which is brought out also with reference to His kingly station. He is 'the ruler of kings on earth' (1:5); He is 'Lord of lords and King of kings' (17:14; 19:16). This is yet another way of associating

Him closely with the Father, for we read in 19:6 that 'the Lord our God the Almighty reigns'. Just how these two sovereignties are related is not worked out, but clearly Christ is thought of as occupying the highest possible place.

Special mention should be made of the seven letters to the churches in chapters 2 and 3. Here we see Christ in the supreme place. He demands the homage of the churches. He praises them where they have done well. He blames them where they have done ill. He assigns to them the rewards they are to receive. In general He assumes the place that God alone can have in the devotion of the churches. He is given some striking name in the address of each of the letters. For example, in the first letter He is 'him who holds the seven stars in his right hand, who walks among the seven golden lampstands' (2:1). In the last verse of the preceding chapter the seven stars are explained as 'the angels of the seven churches', while the lampstands are the churches. This expression then places the churches in His hand. It ascribes to Him the place of Lord of the churches. The addresses are a worthy topic of study, but we can mention only one other, that to the church at Sardis, where we read of Him 'who has the seven spirits of God and the seven stars' (3:1). Again we see the stars with their implications as to His place over the churches. The unusual expression, 'the seven spirits of God' (cf. 5:6), bring Him into close association with the deity.

There is much more, for the nomenclature of Revelation is unusual and very interesting. But even this glimpse is enough to show that the names applied to Jesus reveal a very high view of His Person.

The Lord God and the Lamb

A feature of the last book in the Bible is the way in which the Lamb is associated with God. We read, for example, of 'the throne of God and of the Lamb' (22:3). 'Throne' is singular, which points to something in the nature of joint royalty. We are reminded of the way in which Paul so often does not put a difference between our Lord and the Father. So in the heavenly city, 'the Lord God the Almighty and the Lamb' are the temple (21:22), and they are its light also. More than once 'the word of God' and 'the testimony of Jesus Christ' are linked (1: 2, 9; *cf.* 12:17; 14:12). When we reflect on the unique place that the word of God occupied among the Jews this is a very revealing conjunction. Praise is given to 'him who sits upon the throne and to the Lamb . . . for ever and ever' (5:13), and salvation is ascribed to both (7:10). There is an interesting joint operation, if we may be permitted to put it that way, in 7:17, where 'the Lamb in the midst of the throne' feeds the multitude in white robes, and brings them to the waters, while it is God who wipes away the tears from their eyes.

The writer of this book does not stay to explain the connection between the Lord God and the Lamb. But clearly it is a close one. And just as clearly it is impossible to envisage one who is purely human carrying out the operations ascribed to the Lamb.

It is fascinating to see yet another different way of giving expression to the same great truths that we have seen elsewhere. The highest place in heaven belongs to Him who on earth died for men. In the nature of the case this book which is set in heaven has a great deal more to say about the divine aspect of Jesus than the human. Yet the human is there, too, and it is clear that the seer has in mind One who walked this earth as a man, and who yet was rightly possessed of that place in heaven which can be shared only by the Father and the divine Spirit.

8 Conclusion

Deity is not an easy term to define and throughout this book we have not essayed the task. But it is not impossible to imagine a line which separates God from all God's creatures, so that on one side is God, and on the other is everything less than God. If we ask on which side of this line Jesus Christ is to be found, the answer given by all the New Testament writers is 'God's side'. They differ in their terminology and their habits of thought. They are writing independently. They are not simply copying ideas from one another. Each, as the Spirit of God leads him, gives expression to his own insights into the Person and work of the Lord Jesus. There is great variety in language and in method. When we compare, say, Mark's Gospel with the Letters of Paul, or the writings of Luke with those of John, we are in no doubt that none of these men is simply repeating a stereotyped tale. Each has something to say that matters intensely to him, and he says it in his own way.

All the more impressive is the fundamental agreement which emerges. The great thought of the New Testament is that God has taken action in the Person of His Son to put away man's sin. This is not the idea of one or two writers, but of the whole of the early church. Nowhere in the New Testament do we find any such thought as that Jesus is like one of the angels, or that He can be fully explained in purely human terms. With one accord the New Testament writers insist that Jesus must be thought of as God in the fullest sense. His relationship to the Father is the very closest relationship possible. There is no doubt about the place they ascribe to Jesus.

This is all the more remarkable in view of their convinced monotheism. They do not seem to have envisaged the possibility of a multiplicity of gods. They took it as an axiom that there can be only one God. Without compromise on this basic tenet they yet affirmed the deity of Christ.

This, moreover, is a necessity for Christian thought. Unless Jesus was fully divine our concept of the love of God must suffer. As William Temple put it, 'The wise question is not, "Is Christ Divine?" but, "What is God like?" '[1] If Christ was not God, then in the last resort when men had gone astray, God said in effect, 'I will send someone else to bring them back.' But if Christ was God, He said, 'I will go myself!' It is only the full deity of Christ which enables us to think of God as love, for, 'if Christ was not God saving, He was saving from God.'[2]

At the same time the early church did not waver in its thought that Jesus was a man. It was a man who walked the hills of Galilee and His followers always thought of Him as such. Their preaching must have included this truth, for their converts firmly maintained the reality of Christ's manhood. It is not easy to hold this in conjunction with His deity, and at all times some have found it easier to overbalance into a position which for practical purposes does away with the one or the other.

How these two, the deity and the humanity, are related, or even how they could come to co-exist in the one Person, we do not know. The evidence does not indicate that Jesus was partly God and partly man, that He did some things as God and others as man. Rather He was one Person, though a Person with divine and human characteristics. 'The Person of Jesus does not come apart in our hands into the two halves of humanity and divinity, one of which we have to set on one side when we begin to examine the other. His Personality is a seamless whole.'[3]

The heresies

Since it is difficult to see how one and the same Person can be

[1] *Foundations*, by Seven Oxford Men (London, 1913), p. 259.
[2] P. T. Forsyth, *Positive Preaching and Modern Mind*, p. 252.
[3] H. E. W. Turner, *Jesus Master and Lord* (London, 1953), p. 185.

both God and man it is not suprising that various solutions to the problem have been offered. The possibilities are not many, and the early church ran through them, erroneous solutions being one by one denounced and disowned as heresies. Yet though the defects were made plain in the fires of controversy many of these ideas have been revived in modern times and given a new lease of life. The phrase 'Ancient heresies in modern dress' contains a real truth.

The easiest solution of the problem is simply to shut our eyes to some of the evidence, and this is the pattern of the first heresies to emerge. The Ebionites thought of Jesus as truly a man, but not originally as God, while the Docetists reversed the process. They held that He was God and not man at all. The historical Jesus was something in the nature of a phantom, for the divine Christ could have no real contact with matter. The church promptly disowned both these points of view. Each achieves simplicity at the expense of overlooking much of the relevant evidence.

More serious was the heresy of Arius, a presbyter from Alexandria. He conceived of Jesus along the lines of the pagan demigods, that is as neither God nor man, but as something in between. This view proved enormously popular, and for a time almost captured the church. There was a period when every bishop occupying a see was Arian. But the view is inherently defective. In the first place it is not true to the biblical evidence which regards Jesus as *both* God *and* man. In the second it overlooked the great theological truth that unless Jesus was both God and man the essential basis of our redemption is undermined.

In reaction from Arianism, Apollinarius insisted on the deity of Christ. He thought to solve the problem by thinking of Jesus as a man as regards His body and animal life. But he held that in Jesus the place of the rational soul was taken by the divine Logos. Boettner finds an analogy to this by imagining the implanting of a man's mind in a lion's body, the lion henceforth being governed by human psychology.[1] Apollinarius thought of Jesus as human in His bodily form, but divine in His states of mind and soul. This view, while superficially attractive, does

[1] *Studies in Theology* (Grand Rapids, 1947), p. 263.

violence to the evidence. The Gospels picture for us One who was completely human and completely divine, not a split personality. Moreover, in denying that Jesus assumed the highest part of man's nature Apollinarius struck at His atoning work just as effectively as did Arius. If Jesus did not take our nature upon Him how can He redeem us?

The rejection of Apollinarianism brought recognition that Jesus was possessed of both divine and human natures. But there was still room for speculation as to the way in which these were related. The Nestorians emphasized the manhood of Jesus, and, while they did not overlook His deity, they yet thought of it as the indwelling of the divine within the man Jesus. They held it madness to compare the indwelling of God in Christ with His indwelling in the saints, but the difference seems to have been one of degree rather than kind. In practice this reduced Jesus to being the very greatest of the saints. It is not surprising, accordingly, that once again the church felt constrained to say that this is a view which does violence to the facts.

The swing of the pendulum brought Eutychianism, the view which, in practice, did away with the humanity of Jesus. Eutyches thought of Jesus as having both divine and human natures, but the effect of the conjunction of two such natures was that the human was swallowed up in the divine, like a drop of vinegar in the ocean. The defect in this view, of course, is that it does not allow for a real humanity.

It still needs to be stated plainly and emphatically that no view of the Person of Christ can be regarded as satisfactory which ignores or minimizes either the Godhead or the manhood. In various ways the attempt was made to find some simple solution to the problem. But, plausible though some of these attempts were, each was rightly rejected. They all failed to do justice to the facts recorded in the New Testament, and they failed to do justice to the facts of Christian experience.

If God chooses to become a man for the working out of His purposes, then we must expect that there will be mysteries beyond man's power to solve. But that does not give us licence to shut our eyes to evidence we do not like. There are two main strands in the New Testament. Consistently the New Testament writers think of Jesus as a Jewish man of the first century, but also as One who partook of the essential nature of deity. Naturally the truth of this idea cannot be empirically demonstrated. But we must be quite clear that the New Testament writers held it. It is open to twentieth-century man to reject the biblical evidence and to build his religion on some other foundation. But it is not open to him to accept the New Testament and yet to deny that Jesus was God incarnate.

That should be made clear. But when we have shown that the men of the New Testament held such high views of Jesus there is something further. The faith of these men challenges us to make a similar venture of faith. It is a venture of faith, and no piling up of evidence can make it anything else. The supreme question is still, 'What do you think of the Christ?'